15 days

of prayer with

SAINT JEANNE JUGAN

D0832349

15 days
of prayer series

On a journey, it's good to have a guide. Even great saints took spiritual directors or confessors with them on their itineraries toward sanctity. Now you can be guided by the most influential spiritual figures of all time. The 15 Days of Prayer series introduces their deepest and most personal thoughts.

This popular series is perfect if you are looking for a gift, or if you want to be introduced to a particular guide and his or her spirituality. Each volume contains:

- ॐ A brief biography of the saint or spiritual leader
- ॐ A guide to creating a format for prayer or retreat
- ॐ Fifteen meditation sessions with focus points and reflection guides

15 days

of prayer with

SAINT JEANNE JUGAN

MICHEL LAFON

TRANSLATED BY
LOUISE ASHCROFT

NEW CITY PRESS
Hyde Park, NY

Published in the United States by New City Press
202 Cardinal Rd., Hyde Park, NY 12538
www.newcitypress.com
©2009 New City Press (English translation)

This book is a translation of *Prier 15 Jours avec Jeanne Jugan*,
published by Nouvelle Cité, Montrouge, France.

Cover design by Durva Correia

Library of Congress Cataloging-in-Publication Data:

Lafon, Michel.
  [Prier 15 jours avec Jeanne Jugan. English]
  15 days of prayer with Saint Jeanne Jugan / by Michel Lafon ;
translated by Louise Ashcroft.
      p. cm.
  Includes bibliographical references (p. 139).
  ISBN 978-1-56548-329-3 (pbk. : alk. paper) 1. Jugan, Jeanne, 1792?-
1879—Meditations. 2. Spiritual life—Catholic Church. I. Title. II. Title:
Fifteen days of prayer with Saint Jeanne Jugan.
  BX4700.J77L3413 2009
  242′.76—dc22
                                2009021059

Printed in the United States of America

Contents

How to Use
This Book

*A*n old Chinese proverb, or at least what I am able to recall of what is supposed to be an old Chinese proverb, goes something like this: "Even a journey of a thousand miles begins with a single step." When you think about it, the truth of the proverb is obvious. It is impossible to begin any project, let alone a journey, without taking the first step. I think it might also be true, although I cannot recall if another Chinese proverb says it, "that the first step is often the hardest." Or, as someone else once observed, "the distance between a thought and the corresponding action needed to implement the idea takes the most energy." I don't know who shared that perception with me but I am certain it was not an old Chinese master!

With this ancient proverbial wisdom, and the not-so-ancient wisdom of an unknown contemporary sage still fresh, we move from proverbs to presumptions. How do these relate to the task before us?

I am presuming that if you are reading this introduction it is because you are contemplating a journey. My presumption is that you are preparing for a spiritual journey and that you have taken at least some of the first steps necessary to prepare for this journey. I also presume, and please excuse me if I am making too many presumptions, that in your preparation for the spiritual journey you have determined that you need a guide. From deep within the recesses of your deepest self, there was something that called you to consider Jeanne Jugan as a potential companion. If my presumptions are correct, may I congratulate you on this decision? I think you have made a wise choice, a choice that can be confirmed by yet another source of wisdom, the wisdom that comes from practical experience.

Even an informal poll of experienced travelers will reveal a common opinion; it is very difficult to travel alone. Some might observe that it is even foolish. Still others may be even stronger in their opinion and go so far as to insist that it is necessary to have a guide, especially when you are traveling into uncharted waters and into territory that you have not yet experienced. I am of the personal opinion that a traveling companion is welcome under all circumstances. The thought of traveling alone, to some exciting destination without someone to share the journey with does not capture my imagination or channel my enthusiasm. However, with that being noted, what is simply a matter of preference on the normal journey becomes a matter of necessity when a person embarks on a spiritual journey.

The spiritual journey, which can be the most challenging of all journeys, is experienced best with a guide, a companion, or at the very least, a friend in whom you have placed your trust. This observation is not a preference or an opinion but rather an established spiritual necessity. All of the great saints with whom I am familiar had a spiritual director or a confessor who journeyed with them. Admittedly, at times the saints might well have traveled far beyond the experience of their guide and companion but more often than not they would return to their director and reflect on their experience. Understood in this sense, the director and companion provided a valuable contribution and necessary resource. When I was learning how to pray (a necessity for anyone who desires to be a full-time and public "religious person"), the community of men that I belong to gave me a great gift. Between my second and third year in college, I was given a one-year sabbatical, with all expenses paid and all of my personal needs met. This period of time was called noviatiate. I was officially designated as a novice, a beginner in the spiritual journey, and I was assigned a "master," a person who was willing to lead me. In addition to the master, I was provided with every imaginable book and any other resource that I could possibly need. Even with all that I was provided, I did not learn how to pray because of the books and the unlimited resources, rather it was the master, the companion who was the key to the experience.

One day, after about three months of reading, of quiet and solitude, and of practicing all of the methods and descriptions of prayer that were available to me, the master called. "Put away the books, forget the method, and just listen." We went into a room, became quiet, and tried to recall the presence of God, and then, the master simply prayed out loud and permitted me to listen to his prayer. As he prayed, he revealed his hopes, his dreams, his struggles, his successes, and most of all, his relationship with God. I discovered as I listened that his prayer was deeply intimate but most of all it was self-revealing. As I learned about him, I was led through his life experience to the place where God dwells. At that moment I was able to understand a little bit about what I was supposed to do if I really wanted to pray.

The dynamic of what happened when the master called, invited me to listen, and then revealed his innermost self to me as he communicated with God in prayer, was important. It wasn't so much that the master was trying to reveal to me what needed to be said; he was not inviting me to pray with the same words that he used, but rather that he was trying to bring me to that place within myself where prayer becomes possible. That place, a place of intimacy and of self-awareness, was a necessary stop on the journey and it was a place that I needed to be led to. I could not have easily discovered it on my own.

The purpose of the volume that you hold in your hand is to lead you, over a period of fifteen days or, maybe more realistically, fifteen prayer periods, to a place where prayer is possible. If you already have a regular experience and practice of prayer, perhaps this volume can help lead you to a deeper place, a more intimate relationship with the Lord.

It is important to note that the purpose of this book is not to lead you to a better relationship with Jeanne Jugan, your spiritual companion. Although your companion will invite you to share some of her deepest and most intimate thoughts, your companion is doing so only to bring you to that place where God dwells. After all, the true measurement of all companions for the journey is that they bring you to the place where you need to be, and then they step back, out of the picture. A guide who brings you to the desired destination and then sticks around is a very unwelcome guest!

Many times I have found myself attracted to a particular idea or method for accomplishing a task, only to discover that what seemed to be inviting and helpful possessed too many details. All of my energy went to the mastery of the details and I soon lost my enthusiasm. In each instance, the book that seemed so promising ended up on my bookshelf, gathering dust. I can assure you, it is not our intention that this book end up in your bookcase, filled with promise, but unable to deliver.

There are three simple rules that need to be followed in order to use this book with a measure of satisfaction.

Place: It is important that you choose a place for reading that provides the necessary atmosphere for reflection and that does not allow for too many distractions. Whatever place you choose needs to be comfortable, have the necessary lighting, and, finally, have a sense of "welcoming" about it. You need to be able to look forward to the experience of the journey. Don't travel steerage if you know you will be more comfortable in first class and if the choice is realistic for you. On the other hand, if first class is a distraction and you feel more comfortable and more yourself in steerage, then it is in steerage that you belong.

My favorite place is an overstuffed and comfortable chair in my bedroom. There is a light over my shoulder, and the chair reclines if I feel a need to recline. Once in a while, I get lucky and the sun comes through my window and bathes the entire room in light. I have other options and other places that are available to me but this is the place that I prefer.

Time: Choose a time during the day when you are most alert and when you are most receptive to reflection, meditation, and prayer. The time that you choose is an essential component. If you are a morning person, for example, you should choose a time that is in the morning. If you are more alert in the afternoon, choose an afternoon time slot; and if evening is your preference, then by all means choose the evening. Try to avoid "peak" periods in your daily routine when you know that you might be disturbed. The time that you choose needs to be your time and needs to work for you.

It is also important that you choose how much time you will spend with your companion each day. For some it will be possible to set aside enough time in order to read and reflect on all the material that is offered for a given day. For others, it might not be possible to devote one time to the suggested material for the day, so the prayer period may need to be extended for two, three, or even more sessions. It is not important how long it takes you; it is only important that it works for you and that you remain committed to that which is possible.

For myself I have found that fifteen minutes in the early morning, while I am still in my robe and pajamas and before my morning coffee, and even before I prepare myself for the day, is the best time. No one expects to see me or to interact with me because I have not yet "announced" the fact that I am awake or even on the move. However, once someone hears me in the bathroom, then my window of opportunity is gone. It is therefore important to me that I use the time that I have identified when it is available to me.

Freedom: It may seem strange to suggest that freedom is the third necessary ingredient, but I have discovered that it is most important. By freedom I understand a certain "stance toward life," a "permission to be myself and to be gentle and understanding of who I am." I am constantly amazed at how the human person so easily sets himself or herself up for disappointment and perceived failure. We so easily make judgments about ourselves and our actions and our choices, and very often those judgments are negative, and not at all helpful.

For instance, what does it really matter if I have chosen a place and a time, and I have missed both the place and the time for three days in a row? What does it matter if I have chosen, in that twilight time before I am completely awake and still a little sleepy, to roll over and to sleep for fifteen minutes more? Does it mean that I am not serious about the journey, that I really don't want to pray, that I am just fooling myself when I say that my prayer time is important to me? Perhaps, but I prefer to believe that it simply means that I am tired and I just wanted a little more sleep. It doesn't mean anything more than that. However, if I make it mean more than that, then I can become discouraged, frustrated, and put myself into a state where I might more easily give up. "What's the use? I might as well forget all about it."

The same sense of freedom applies to the reading and the praying of this text. If I do not find the introduction to each day helpful, I don't need to read it. If I find the questions for reflection at the end of the appointed day repetitive, then I should choose to close the book and go my own way. Even if I discover that the reflection offered for the day is not the one that I prefer and that the one for the next day seems more inviting, then by all means, go on to the one for the next day.

That's it! If you apply these simple rules to your journey you should receive the maximum benefit and you will soon find yourself at your destination. But be prepared to be surprised. If you have never been on a spiritual journey you should know that the "travel brochures" and the other descriptions that you might have heard are nothing compared to the real thing. There is so much more than you can imagine.

A final prayer of blessing suggests itself:

Lord, catch me off guard today.
Surprise me with some moment of
       beauty or pain
So that at least for the moment
I may be startled into seeing that you
   are here in all your splendor,
Always and everywhere,
Barely hidden,
Beneath,
Beyond,
Within this life I breathe.

Frederick Buechner

Rev. Thomas M. Santa, CSsR
Liguori, Missouri

A Brief Chronology of Jeanne Jugan's Life

*T*he 15 days of prayer proposed in this book make reference to events in the life of Jeanne Jugan, foundress of the Little Sisters of the Poor. The following dates give an overview of her life.

October 25, 1792:
> Birth of Jeanne in Cancale (Ille-et-Vilaine). She is baptized the same day.

1796: Her father is lost at sea.

1810: Jeanne works as a kitchen maid at the Château de la Mettrie-aux-Chouettes.

1816: A mission is preached in Cancale. Jeanne decides to dedicate herself entirely to God and refuses a marriage proposal from a young sailor. *"God wants me for himself."*

> She leaves her family to live in Saint Servan, near Saint-Malo, where she works at Le Rosais Hospital.

Jeanne enters the Third Order of the Admirable Mother, founded in the 17th century by St. Jean Eudes. She makes a vow of perpetual chastity.

1823: She leaves Le Rosais Hospital and is welcomed into the home of Miss Lecoq, more as a friend than as a maid. Together the two women visit the poor and study the catechism.

1833: Arrival of the Brothers of St. John of God at Dinan.

1835: Miss Lecoq dies, leaving Jeanne a modest inheritance. Jeanne continues to work for some well-to-do families.

1837: With her friend Françoise Aubert, Jeanne rents an apartment in a house on rue du Centre called the *Mansarde*. Françoise spins and Jeanne works during the day.

An 18-year-old orphan, Virginie Tréda-niel, moves in and helps Jeanne with her work.

Winter 1839:

In agreement with Françoise Aubert, Jeanne takes in a blind and infirm elderly woman, Anne Chauvin, for whom she gives up her bed. Another poor woman, Isabelle Coeuru, is welcomed into their care shortly afterwards.

1840: Marie Jamet assists Jeanne and Virginie. The three women form an association, with a simple Rule inspired by the Third Order of St. Eudes. Father Le Pailleur, assistant priest of the parish of Saint-Servan, is delegated by his parish priest to watch over their initiative.

1841: Jeanne, her companions and guests move into the ground floor of a building on rue de la Fontaine, spacious enough to accommodate twelve beds. Jeanne starts collecting. *"I was the little beggar. I asked and held out my hand."*

May 29, 1842:
At a meeting of the "Servants of the Poor," in the presence of Father Le Pailleur, Jeanne is elected Superior.

September 1842:
Acquisition of the old convent of the Daughters of the Cross as a home for the elderly. The dormitories are arranged and the first man, poverty-stricken Rodolphe Laisné, in his seventies and abandoned in a hovel, is welcomed. Jeanne continues her collections and pays back loans.

December 1843:
On December 8, Jeanne is re-elected Superior. On December 23, Father Le Pailleur annuls the election and names

Marie Jamet to replace her. He declares himself founder of the association and secures for himself the position of Father Superior General. Jeanne, 51, steps down without complaining, making way for the twenty-three-year-old Superior. *"If God places a child in place of the first Superior, I will obey him."*

1845: Jeanne is awarded the Montyon Prize by the French Academy for her work.

1846: Jeanne works on the foundation of a house in Rennes, followed by another in Dinan.

1847: On the request of Mr. Dupont, "the Holy Man of Tours," the Sisters establish a house in Tours. Jeanne is requested every-where as soon as any problem arises; she makes contact with the civil and religious authorities and seeks possible accommo-dations and benefactors.

1850: In Angers, Jeanne accomplishes her last foundation. The Little Sisters number over one hundred, including novices and postulants.

1852: Diocesan approbation of the Institute by Monseigneur Brossais Saint-Marc, bishop of Rennes. The Motherhouse returns to Rennes. Marie Jamet and Virginie Trédaniel make their perpetual vows;

Jeanne Jugan is authorized to do so only two years later on December 8. Jeanne is recalled to the Motherhouse where she is relieved of all responsibility and activity.

1856: The Motherhouse and novitiate move to the estate of La Tour, in the commune of Saint-Pern (Ille-et-Vilaine). Jeanne Jugan joins them, beginning her definitive retirement, and lives among the novices and postulants. *"I no longer see anything but the good God."*

1866: The Saint-Servan town council name a street after Jeanne Jugan.

1867: The one-hundredth house of the Congregation is founded. Addressing Father Le Pailleur one day, Jeanne jokingly lets slip, *"My good Father, you have stolen my work from me, but I give it to you willingly."*

March 1, 1879:

Pope Leo XIII approves the Constitutions of the Congregation.

August 29, 1879:

Sister Mary of the Cross (Jeanne Jugan) dies at the age of 86 and is buried on the same day in the cemetery of the Little Sisters at La Tour Saint-Joseph. At this time, the Congregation numbers 2,488 nuns in 177 houses welcoming approximately 20,500 elderly persons.

June 1890:

The Holy See summons Father Le Pailleur to Rome, where he spends his final years in a convent.

1936: The body of Jeanne Jugan is transferred to the crypt of the Motherhouse chapel.

1970: The Cause of Jeanne Jugan is officially introduced by a decree of the Congregation for the Causes of Saints.

October 3, 1982:

Jeanne Jugan is beatified by Pope John Paul II. Her feast day is celebrated on August 30.

Today pilgrims can visit the sites where St. Jeanne Jugan lived: the house where she was born (Cancale), the "Mansarde" and the House of the Cross (Saint-Servan), as well as La Tour Saint Joseph, the Motherhouse of the Little Sisters, where Jeanne Jugan spent the last twenty-three years of her life.

October 11, 2009:

Jeanne Jugan is canonized by Pope Benedict XVI.

Introduction

$\int$ aint Jeanne Jugan left us neither letters nor writings, not a single line apart from her signature at the end of an official document. This clearly poses a serious problem for those wishing to explore and meditate on her spirituality. When we began gathering testimony on her life, we interviewed some elderly nuns who had frequented Jeanne Jugan towards the end of her life over fifty years earlier. Many of those who had known her during her active period had long since departed for paradise. No writings and only a few words bear witness to the supreme consecration of an entire life marked by poverty and humility.

Nevertheless, earlier witnesses had left us with their memories of her actions and gestures, among them the "Holy Man of Tours" Mr. Leo Dupont, authors Louis Veuillot and Charles Dickens, as well as several women religious and members of the laity. These testimonies, along with rare archival material, have enabled us to reconstitute the story of the beginnings of the

Congregation of the Little Sisters of the Poor and Jeanne Jugan's role in its founding.

On reading these descriptive accounts about her, and imagining the places that bore witness to her life, love, prayers, and suffering; in gathering the least of her words, and through being in constant contact with her, I was surprised to find myself conversing with her. Believing I knew her a little, I permitted myself to give her a voice, trying to make her as alive for the reader as she has become for me.

As far back as Plato, writers have imagined dialogues with people from the beyond. Christian authors were no exception and did not hesitate to portray Jesus and his words in works from *The Imitation of Christ* to authors such as Pascal and Charles de Foucauld. These prestigious predecessors — with whom, I assure you, I cannot compare myself — have, however, paved the way for me to present you with this book of meditation in the form of dialogues with Jeanne Jugan. Although imagined, these dialogues are not implausible. They came to me through the personality and work of Jeanne Jugan. Included among the words I have given her are her own words, as told by her contemporaries for the purpose of her beatification: differences in the typeface make this distinction clear.

Throughout the exchange I call her my Sister, and ask her to call me *my Brother* instead of *Father* or *Reverend* (terms which seem contrary to the spirit of the Gospel to me). Of course, addressing a priest as a brother was not typical in her day, but she adapted to it very well!

Poverty is the thread tying together her whole existence, and it is this that Cardinal Garrone developed in his book *Poor in Spirit*. Closely linked to poverty was her striving for littleness, a virtue to which Jesus invites us, which is portrayed in Jeanne's life and which makes her a kindred spirit to St. Thérèse of Lisieux. Her unfailing faith in Providence, which she passed on to the Little Sisters, and, like St. John of God and other Saints, her conviction that "the poor are Our Lord" are driven by her deep love of Our Lord Jesus. Her spirituality is Christocentric, even though she often speaks of the *Good God*, like many in her day. These traits of her spiritual physiognomy are implied in everything that is said about her, so one should not be surprised if a theme touched on in one chapter is revisited in another way since her life is unified around several essential axes. Where I have employed Jeanne Jugan's use of "my" to refer to the elderly and poor does not denote any kind of possessiveness on her part but a sense of being a member of the same family. I have also retained her use of "good," a term of affection she used to refer to the elderly, God and Mother, which some may find somewhat high and mighty, but was used by her in its true sense, meaning good or full of goodness, which is close to the divine!

I hope with all my heart that I have brought St. Jeanne Jugan to life in these pages as she speaks to us through her humble life and words. I also hope that after listening to her you the reader will say a "good" little prayer for the one who ventured into conversation with her with no regrets!

* * *

The themes of the fifteen days you will spend with Jeanne Jugan are linked together as follows:

The first day evokes God's calling, the beginning of her vocation.

Day Two explores her lifelong conviction that the "poor are Our Lord," and Day Three the consequence of this, the themes of welcoming and hospitality.

Days Four and Five meditate on the spiritual facets of having nothing and depending on God for everything.

Day Six develops the theme of littleness, an aspect of spiritual poverty, joining to it the spirit of childhood.

The collecting is discussed on Day Seven, followed on Day Eight by the triple presence of God: in us, in the poor, and in the tabernacle.

Suggestions on how to live one's daily life are explored over several days: Day Nine by blessing God, Day Ten by acting through love, Day Eleven by believing in our weakness and the strength of God, and Day Twelve by welcoming the cross that unites us with Christ.

Day Thirteen explains three maxims from the Scriptures that were dear to Jeanne Jugan.

Day Fourteen is dedicated to the Holy Family, in particular to the devotion to St. Joseph, for whom the Little Sisters of the Poor have a special devotion.

And finally, Day Fifteen illustrates the importance of the Virgin Mary in the life and death of Jeanne Jugan.

Michel Lafon

Note on the typeface:
All the words I place on the lips of Jeanne Jugan are reproduced in *italics*, whereas authentic quotes, gathered from her fellow Sisters, are reproduced in **bold**. These witness accounts all originate from the *Positio super virtutibus*, compiled in view of Jeanne Jugan's beatification, published by the Vatican in 1976.

See Bibliography for references.

1
God Wants Me for Himself

Focus Point

////////////

God has a plan for each of us. As the well-known prayer of John Henry Newman says, "God has created me to do him some definite service; he has committed some work to me which he has not committed to another. I have my mission … " Whether it be discerning our life's vocation when we are young, or just having an intuition of what he is asking of us on a particular day, God is always speaking to us and giving us subtle signs to reveal his will for us. He speaks through persons and events — he speaks in the depths of our hearts. Let us pray for a listening heart and for the generosity to receive each invitation from God with the openness of Mary: "I am the servant of the Lord; let it be done to me according to your word."

////////////

"God wants me for himself. He is keeping me for a work which is not yet founded."

"Go everywhere praising God."

— When you were 18 years old, my Sister, you were asked for your hand in marriage by a young sailor who had noticed you and who seemed not to displease you, as one used to say. Yet you hesitated to make a commitment and asked him to wait. With hope in his heart, he left for sea ...

— *You know, even if he had received my consent, our engagement would have lasted several years. That was the tradition in Cancale at the time.*

— What did your parents say?

— *My father died before I was four. He was a fisherman and was among the many men of Cancale to be lost at sea. My mother found my suitor acceptable, but I felt I needed to be there for her and continue to work close to my family.*

— What kind of work were you doing?

— *I started by looking after the troops on the high cliffs dominating the bay of Cancale, by spinning, knitting, or by saying my rosary. I could not stop contemplating the sea, its sheer immensity, its changing colors, and the movements of its waves. It was undoubtedly then that I got into the habit of thanking God while contemplating all the beauty of creation. Towards the end of my life, I enjoyed walk-*

ing in the garden at La Tour Saint-Joseph, admiring the flowers. Opening the window on a winter morning to discover the countryside under a blanket of snow is simply magnificent! It is all God's creation. He who loves us and whom we love. I said over and over again, "Blessed be God!" and asked the novices to continue to do the same.

Following my first communion, I worked for several years for the viscountess at the Château de La Mettrie-aux-Chouettes in the commune of Saint-Coulomb. It wasn't too far from home, about five kilometers away: how many times I made that journey on foot! The viscountess was very kind and asked me to visit the many poor people of the village. I remember the elderly fishermen who were infirm and deprived of resources. There were also beggars who came knocking at the door of the mansion.

— What became of the sailor who wished to marry you?

— He demonstrated great patience as I continued to postpone my decision. It was during that time (1816) that a three-week parish mission was held at Cancale. You can't imagine what this event meant for the whole population. Over twenty priests came for the sermons, exercises and mission celebrations. The church was packed. I was swept up by this wave of fervor, and one fine day, I felt the deep conviction that **God wanted me for himself**. And slowly but surely, this conviction became so strong that I confided in *my mother what I felt so clearly,* **"God wants me for himself. He is keeping me for a work that is not yet founded."** *It was God that had given me this certainty. My conviction had come from him. How else could I have had such an idea? My mother and sisters were a little concerned, but my feeling was so profound, so strong within me that I told them I would never marry. To the man who still regarded me as his fiancée, I declared that he must renounce his hopes for me since God wanted me for himself. His call had become irresistible and I was certain I was not wrong. Later, priests confirmed me in my conviction.*

— The Lord had a mission for you. Does he not have one for each and every one of us? At each turning point in our lives, should we not ask ourselves what the Lord expects from us? In childhood, on the day of my first communion, the Lord made me understand internally that he wished me to become a missionary. It never occurred to me to question this calling even though I couldn't imagine exactly what it meant. The paths on which God leads us are unforeseeable and sometimes disconcerting.

— *I welcomed God's calling into my heart, but you know, dear Brother, I did so without knowing where this would lead me. I had no idea.*

— This is the way of the Lord. He shows us the light for us to make the first steps, but he does not enlighten us in advance as to the rest of the journey. What he wants from us reveals itself the further we advance. We must let him guide us in total confidence. Only he knows the way.

— *The year after the great mission, my sister, Thérèse-Charlotte, who was younger than I by two years, married a sailor from Cancale. It was then that I made the painful decision to leave the house where I was born to work at Le Rosais Hospital in Saint-Servan. I cried a great deal, but my decision freed me, making me more available to fulfil God's will, which had still not revealed itself to me.*

— And at Saint-Servan, you joined the Third Order of the Admirable Mother, founded by St. John Eudes.

— *Yes, this gave me the spiritual guidance that I was missing. Don't forget what I had experienced during the Revolution. The first Constitutions of the Little Sisters (1852) were greatly inspired by the regulations of the Third Order.*

The red silk insignia of the members represented the hearts of Jesus and Mary, one mounted on a cross, the other pierced through. We had a devotion towards the Blessed Virgin Mary; we wished to greet and honor her, choosing her as "advocate and refuge for all our needs," while "uniting ourselves with all hearts in heaven and on earth that love this dearest Mother." All of the virtues that we extolled were in imitation of the heart of the Holy Virgin and, above all, of the love of God.

— Today, although we do not use the same language as in your youth, we can still follow in the footsteps of the Virgin Mary in her attitude of acceptance: "I am the servant of the Lord. May it be done to me as you have said." The Virgin Mary was the first to receive, through the intermediary of an angel, a calling from God, who also wanted her for himself. And you, my Sister, you followed in her faithful footsteps by answering "Yes" to the call of God, and by making a perpetual vow of chastity. On the day of the Annunciation, the Virgin Mary did not know that this road would lead her to Calvary; she only wanted to be a servant of the Lord. You also did not know that the road to Saint-Servan would mean that you would be kept in the background of the work you initiated, painful though this was. And, among the poor of your times, you, like Mary, were a servant of God.

Reflection Questions

Am I a good listener? Do I take time out to listen to the voice of God speaking to my heart? Am I afraid of silence? Of prayer? Am I familiar with God's word and his ways, as Mary was? Do I take advantage of opportunities for growing in my relationship with God, for growing in faith? Do I believe that God acts through others, and through the daily circumstances of my life? Are my eyes open to discern his presence in my daily life? Am I open to his plans for me, even when they differ from my own? Am I too attached to my own way, to certain possessions or plans? Do I sometimes lack the courage or generosity to follow his will, even when it is clear to me, or do I go ahead, trusting in his personal love for me? God wants each of us for himself.

2
The Poor Are Our Lord

Focus Point

////////////

Jesus promised that we will always have the poor with us. But he went even further than that, identifying himself with the poor: "Whatever you did for the least of these brothers of mine, you did for me." Seeing Jesus in those who suffer is a matter of faith; loving them is a measure of our love for God himself. Lord, give us eyes of faith and hearts ready to love you in the poor.

////////////

"In serving the aged, it is he himself whom you are serving ... They are the suffering members of Our Lord."

"Look upon the poor with compassion, and Jesus will look upon you with kindness on your last day."

"Be kind, especially with the infirm. Love them well ... Oh yes! Be kind."

"The spirit of faith consists of speaking to our brothers as if we were speaking to another Jesus Christ."

— In the past, the poor of Saint-Servan were reduced to begging under difficult conditions. In 1832, the municipality was presented with a report on "the eradication of begging." As a result, the city was divided into 18 quarters, with two women designated to each one to "find out about the unfortunate and provide for their needs." At the time, you could not foresee what your role would be in this fight against poverty. Twelve years later, the mayor declared that pauperism was only increasing: "Since 1844, 4,500 of the hungry needy in a population of 9,700 were served by the Charity Office." During this time, you were welcoming and taking care of "a family of sixty-five poverty-stricken men and women, all elderly, infirm, or crippled ... , all protected in your care from misery and the shame of begging in the streets" (Memoire for the French Academy).

In our day, the vocabulary we use to refer to the aged has changed. We no longer say "little old men or women" but rather the elderly, aged or senior citizens. We also speak of the lack of security, of exclusion, and marginalization. All around us, many people are suffering both materially and morally. One only needs to evoke the plight of refugees, the jobless, those suffering from cancer or AIDS …

My Sister, You taught us to be good, tirelessly good. This is very demanding.

— *If we think of the words of Jesus, "Whatever you did for one of the least of these brothers of mine, you did for me," this will help us to serve the poor. We should see Jesus in the aged, for they speak of the Good Lord.* Through them it is God that is calling us.

— I was looking at the painting in your chapel at La Tour Saint-Joseph, which evokes what you just said. In it, John of God is washing the feet of a poor man who is transformed into Jesus, and whom the Saint recognizes. Jesus confirms softly to him, "John, all the good that you do for the poor in my name, you do to me … I am dressed in the clothes with which you cover them, and you wash my feet whenever you wash those of the poor and the sick." Seeing Jesus in those who suffer depends on our faith. Of course we can see what our eyes show us, but if our faith is strong, we see beyond this with a piercing regard, a kind of second sight, which sees the invisible. The Epistle to the Hebrews tells us that "Moses persevered because he saw him who was invisible" (Heb 11:27). This is a truly magnificent definition of faith!

Seeing with the eyes of faith means regarding the other through God's eyes and not just through our own experience of what we see and hear; it means not only looking at what seems to be but also at what is. In other words, it means seeing the other as God sees him. This can help us when we are faced with barriers of nationalism and religion, and certainly when we feel we have been slighted or others have an antipathy toward us — Jesus asks us to love our enemies.

In his description of the Last Judgment, Jesus speaks of those who are hungry and thirsty, of those who are sick or imprisoned. Personally, I go to them simply because they are suffering. I want to help them in their distress, and love them for their own sake ... And in the same movement, Jesus himself is touched by my words and actions. My faith has helped me to rise above any obstacles but it has never reduced my fraternal charity to a means to something else: I do not practice charity so that I will be looked upon favorably from heaven! When I give a present to a child, for example, it is to make the child happy, yet often the child's mother is equally happy as if she had received the gift herself. In this way, Jesus empathizes with the smallest of his brothers. When I give food to the hungry, I do so because they are hungry, but this gesture results in a twofold joy — for the one who has been fed and for the One who identifies himself with him.

— I always loved the poor because I loved the dear Lord who is infinitely good to everyone. In the Gospel according to St. Matthew, Jesus asks us to imitate God's kindness so that we "may be sons of your Father in heaven. He causes his sun to rise on the evil and the good, and sends rain on the righteous and the unrighteous" (Mt 5:45). Never will we be good enough. This is something I have always said.

— This is the awful truth, my dear Sister. As Jesus says in the passage you just quoted, we must imitate our Lord in Heaven: "You, therefore, must be perfect, as your heavenly Father is perfect." This obviously means placing our ideals at the highest level.

This demand is understandable if we contemplate the words of God in the Bible: "Let us make man in our image, in our likeness" (Gen 1:26). This is why the more we are good, the more we resemble God. Beyond our weaknesses and selfishness, kindness reflects the divine in our hearts and makes us into the human beings that God wishes us to be. The great philosopher Jacques Maritain said of this subject, "An act of true kindness, the slightest act of real kindness, is the best proof of the existence of God. Yet our intelligence is too encumbered by preconceived notions for us to see him." What is certain is that God is Love: Love is the definition of God, inasmuch as one can define the unknowable.

At the core of humanity, even at the root of life itself, there is love, since it is God himself who makes us spring up, who breathes life into us … and fills us with himself, he who is Love. We recognize this when Jesus introduces the parable of the Good Samaritan. Addressing the scribe who is questioning him, Jesus tells him that the answer is in the Law and is the first of the commandments: "Love the Lord your God with all your heart, with all your soul, with all your strength and with all your mind. Love your neighbor as yourself." In this love, our neighbor is inseparable from God; they are one and the same. Jesus says, "Do this and you will live" (Lk 10: 26–28). If we join these two commandments together, what they say is, "If you love, you will live." To live is to love — what an admirable destiny for humankind! In this regard, I cannot resist citing Maurice Bellet, who evokes this love which is so unselfish and gratuitous: "It joins the One who is extremely humble, God himself, who is the source of all things. It is he who illuminates life itself."

The cross is the sign of this love selflessly given, divested of all thirst for power, in total destitution … The passion of our Lord unfolds over time, but the resurrection is constantly superimposed. In the Eucharist, we worship his body given up for us, and at the same time the glorious body of the Risen One, total love and the triumph of life over death …

Acts of true kindness, no matter how small, have such a divine source, they make us see God!

— *Do not forget that at the end of time, everyone will be judged on what they have done for their neighbor: "I was sick and you took care of me … Whatever you did for one of the least of these brothers of mine, you did for me."* **You must be very kind when caring for the poor, it is so consoling to think that it is for the person of Our Lord himself. You mustn't be afraid of putting a bit of effort into doing the cooking well, just as for looking after them well when they are sick … For those who never think to thank you for all you do for them, say in your heart, "It is for you, my Jesus." Look upon the poor with compassion and Jesus will look upon you with kindness on your last day.**

— On Judgment Day, there will be joyful surprises for those who have been good in their daily lives, and great celebration when we see all these Samaritans lined up together. For good reason, Jesus chose the Samaritan, a heretic held in contempt by his countrymen, as the hero of his parable. The injured man and those listening to Jesus were made to recognize that the person who showed himself closest to the injured man was the one furthest from him in spirit and heart. Obviously, the injured man at the side of the road was Jesus. Nobody knew it, but on the last day one will discover the

Samaritan standing in wonder and the others in shame. Meanwhile, let us ask ourselves these questions: Who are our Samaritans? And on the side of the road, where is Jesus?

Lord Jesus, help us see beyond appearances! Let us see with faith, and give us an indefatigably good heart!

Reflection Questions

Where is Jesus hiding in my milieu? Who are "the poor" in whom Jesus disguises himself, that I may respond? Do I have eyes to see them? Do I make the effort to reach out? Do I perform acts of charity for a pure motive, or do I look for some reward? Do I really believe that God is love, and that he expects a response of love from me in return for all he as done for me? Do I experience acts of charity as life-giving?

3
You Must Always Be Cheerful

Focus Point

////////////

Joy is a fruit of love and a sure sign of God's presence in the soul. It is love that enables us to be joyful, even in the midst of suffering, for it is love that enables us to put our own needs and desires aside in order to bring the Good News to others, to make them happy. Lord, teach us to smile through love.

////////////

"Making the poor happy, that's what counts."

"You must always be cheerful. Our elderly do not like long faces."

— The three usual vows taken by those committing themselves to a religious life are poverty, chastity, and obedience. You, my Sister, added hospitality.

— *From the first years, I was advised and encouraged by Father Massot, from the Brothers of St. John of God. In Dinan, there was an extremely fervent community of these brothers, who had made a vow of hospitality. My companions and I received a diploma that certified our union and allowed us to "participate in the merits, prayers and good works" of this charitable order. They represented important spiritual support for us. How could we not be inspired by the example of their founding Saint? As he and his brothers welcomed the sick, we would welcome the elderly. At that time, we were living in the House of the Cross, and the four of us had just chosen our religious names (from then on I would be known as Mary of the Cross). Three days later, on February 7, 1844, we walked in procession towards the statue of the Virgin Mary. Lit only by the flame of our candles, we made our vows of poverty and hospitality for the first time.*

— I read in the Constitutions of the Little Sisters that "each one in the community brings her collaboration to the common tasks, always in humility, good understanding and peace, so as to radiate the joy born of the practice of hospitality" (*Constitutions,* 59). Consequently, for a Little Sister, joy is not separate from hospitality. Is a welcome still a welcome without a smile? You, my dear Sister, were joyful. At the end of your life, while you walked the corridors of the novitiate and the paths of the garden, you liked to sing hymns to the novices and teach them little refrains. Your Sisters said that you were "always smiling" and that you had a "joyful heart." I was pleased to hear this since your rare portraits are a little severe! It's true that long peregrinations for the collecting and constant rebuffs do not predispose one to gaiety. I've heard a story about a slap in the face you received.

— *A man from Dinan, whom I asked for alms for the elderly I was taking care of, was so annoyed by my insistence that he gave me a slap in the face. Without being discouraged, I turned the other cheek, as the Lord asks us to do, saying, "That was for me, but now, Sir, you will give me something good for my poor?"*

— My Sister, you reacted with such good humor; this must have helped calm the man down. Besides, witnesses even say that this exchange led to his conversion.

I think that we must ask for the grace of humor, so that we never dramatize what is happening to us and preserve a certain distance from the event in question. All too often, we get caught up in our emotions and our judgment becomes clouded. In such cases, we need a "contemplative distance" to maintain our sense of perspective and prevent us from taking things too seriously. Humor — is it not a lifelong program — this word that begins with humility and ends with love? Humility makes us accept our troubles joyfully because the love of our brothers is stronger than that which frustrates us. Since love is at its origin, one must not confuse humor with any old joke or witticism, even less with irony, which is so often hurtful. "Humor is said to be the amused smile of love."

— *It's true. It's important to always smile. It's not always easy with people who are suffering or with those who are bitter. Only love can help us to overcome brusque reactions and* **always be cheerful***. I liked to hear the novices sing what I called "The Song of the Cheerful Face," whose words were quite something! I won't break into song, just quote a few lines: The cheerful face and the little smile … Always be small, never susceptible, etc. It is about practicing the love that St. Paul praises when he wrote, "Love is patient, love is kind … it is not easily angered, it keeps no record of wrongs. It always protects, always trusts, always hopes, always perseveres" (1 Cor 13:4–7).*

— Such love, in daily life, creates a peaceful and happy climate for the aged. It does not prevent one from taking initiatives that will bring unexpected pleasures — on the contrary. When I was a child, we used to give each other surprises, which we prepared in secret. The fact that someone would receive a surprise added a particular sense of joy for each of us. You also gave surprises — I even read that one day you even invited a group of musicians!

— In our homes, I liked the fact that we celebrated birthdays with good dinners inasmuch as we could. **And Saint Joseph was pleased to see his protégés well taken care of!** *But man does not live on bread alone. Celebrating is not only about the pleasure of food but also about the spirit. At Angers, for one birthday, I went to see the colonel of the regiment and asked him to send some musicians to cheer up our Residents, to which he replied, "Sister, I will send you the whole band to bring pleasure and joy to you and your elderly." Which he did, and you should have seen how happy this made everyone — the musicians and the Residents! You know, Bringing joy to the poor is one of my refrains.*

— Bringing joy to the poor: we can extend this to everyone the Lord places on our path in life. Making the other happy — is this not a definition of love in the life of a couple or a family? And then we can extend this to all to whom we are close. Making the other happy, at all costs, even if this means sacrificing our time, money, or love. And this can begin in early childhood: instead of completing a task out of fear of punishment, why not offer positive motivation, for example "to make mommy happy." This means learning to love, to think about others, and to leave our ego aside ... And this leads us to the famous golden rule of the Gospel, "So in everything, do to others what you would have them do to you, for this sums up the Law and the Prophets" (Mt 7:12).

At every Mass, Jesus invites us to his table, and in Communion, we welcome him joyfully into our hearts. This hospitality must be extended outside of the church. How can we receive him in the reverence of the Eucharist and then shut the door in his face when he presents himself in the form of those who suffer all around us? Is he not the same when he presents himself to us in the form of bread and wine?

Lord, teach us to smile with love. It will take time to learn, but this will be good for everyone! And please, give us a sense of humor — this would be a welcome surprise for everyone around us, and I believe this would also please the angels!

Reflection Questions

What is my greatest source of joy? Do I find my joy in God? Is the Gospel really "good news" for me? Am I able to set aside my own needs in order to make others happy? Do I have a good sense of humor? Can I laugh at myself and at life's unexpected twists and turns? Do I know how to share my joy with others?

4
Poverty Is
My Treasure

Focus Point

////////////

There is more to poverty than meets the eye.
That so many of our brothers and sisters live
below the poverty line is a real and inexcusable
injustice. At the same time, Jeanne Jugan said
that it is beautiful to be poor; and Jesus extolled
those who embrace spiritual poverty, promising
them the Kingdom of Heaven. Clearly Gospel
poverty is different. When freely chosen, poverty
is an expression of love — we choose poverty in
imitation of Jesus who was poor, and we love
the poor because Jesus himself loves them. Lord,
give us poor hearts, hearts open to share.

////////////

*"If you want to please the Good Lord, you
must love poverty."*

"The Blessed Virgin was poor; she acted as the poor would and taught us about poverty … Here, our little family must resemble the Holy Family. »

"We were very poor, but we were happy."

— We often cite the following saying: "**It is so good to be poor, to have nothing, to depend on God for everything.**" And sometimes, we reproduce the first seven words and separate them from what follows. My first reflex, I have to admit, my dear Sister, is to leap up with indignation. I understand what you are trying to say, but …

— *Yes, what is important is exactly what follows the first part: that **it is good to depend on God for everything.***

— One must acknowledge that "it is good to be poor" requires some explanation. No, it is never good to be poor. Millions of people all over the world live in desperate poverty, and this is terrible. In fact, what you wanted since you started your work was to reduce poverty and free people from their misery. You started with the blind and infirm Anne Chauvin, and continued with Isabelle Coeuru. Did you not carry Anne on your back and give up your bed for her? You gave these poor women the basic necessities of life of which they had been deprived. Your work was in response to an

unacceptable situation that reduced the poor
to begging. And your refuge at Saint-Servan
for the elderly, most of whom were saved from
beggary, was officially recognized. Your work
repaired the injustice of society: these people
needed to be saved from poverty; in the face of
indifference and rejection, they needed to be
given back their dignity.

— *When my companions and I welcomed our
first elderly,* **we slept on straw, happy in the knowledge that the elderly had beds to sleep in.**

— It's true, you lived among the poor for
whom you cared. You did not wish to be superior to them and treated them as though you
were their "little sister." The memoire addressed
to the French Academy refers to the first years
of your work: "This girl," — it is you they are
talking about — "truly identifies her lot with the
poor. She dresses like them in clothes given to
her; she — like them — eats leftovers, always
careful to save the best for those who are sick or
more needy; and those who help her follow her
example." When Mr. Dupont, the Holy Man of
Tours, visited you, he noticed that you ate the
"same food as the poor" with whom you shared
your life.

— *This is how everything began. At Saint-
Servan, I was in the habit of visiting the poor and
doing what I could for them. I found it normal to
love the poor since I loved the dear Lord. One day,*

I asked my confessor to teach me how to love God better. "Jeanne," he said, "up until now, you have given to the poor. From now on, share with them. The town is full of destitute and infirm elderly women … Welcome one of these poor women into your home; feed her, serve her, console her, talk to her of Heaven. In this way, you will love God more than ever." This is why I welcomed Anne into our home.

— The consequence of sharing rather than just giving meant living in poverty. You gave up your bed and slept on straw … And at the Charity Office, you stood in line with them; you were one of the poor.

— *You can speak of sharing if you like, but think of the multiplication of the loaves told in the Gospel. All of the bread that the Apostles gave to Jesus's hungry followers came from the Lord, since the apostles had neither food nor money to give them. They were, however, able to use their hands to share the food among the hungry. It was the same for us. We had nothing to feed the poor, whom we received in great numbers.*

— That reminds me of something beautiful that Mr. Dupin said at the French Academy when you were awarded the Montyon Prize: "The virtue that shines in Jeanne to an eminent degree is that she gave so much yet had nothing." Is this not the ultimate form of sharing?

— *At times it was hard, and I encouraged the Little Sisters, saying, "If we knew how to under-*

stand the wealth that we have for Heaven, how much we would love our old mended dresses and our poor food!"

— Indeed, my Sister. When we consider that what we possess does not belong to us, and that, before God, we are just there to manage these things and to use them for the good of others, we become the poor that the Lord blessed: "Blessed are the poor in spirit, for theirs is the kingdom of Heaven" (Mt 5:3).

— *When I speak of poverty, my Brother, it is exactly this evangelical poverty that I have in mind; it is this that is beautiful and this is my treasure. And don't forget,* **"Our Lord was poor, and so was the Blessed Virgin, and that's why I too wanted to be poor until my dying day."**

— Dear Sister, many times you have contemplated the life of Our Lord Jesus from the cradle to the cross. At his birth, he lay in a manger full of straw, a vulnerable infant in the simplest of surroundings; the first who came to worship him were shepherds, who at that time were at the bottom of the social ladder and were often looked down upon.

— *When I belonged to the Third Order of St. John Eudes, we were taught to live the mysteries of Jesus Christ. At Christmas, we were asked to transport ourselves in spirit to the stable in Bethlehem and to take our place among the shepherds to worship the divine infant. While contemplating him, we learned the practice of humility, gentleness, and the spirit of poverty.*

— For the whole of his public life, Jesus, a former carpenter, refused to settle down in one place. He moved from village to village without a fixed place to rest his head. And on the cross, between two thieves, stripped of his clothes and his honor, condemned, abandoned by his disciples — what supreme poverty! This is the life that God chose for him of his own free will, in his sovereign liberty! We understand that men and women through the centuries have voluntarily lived in poverty in imitation of Jesus Christ — St. Francis of Assisi and Charles de Foucauld. The admirable Christian Blaise Pascal wrote, " I like poverty because he loved it," and added, "I love material things because they provide the means to assist the wretched" (Brunschvicg, 550).

This thought contains the two elements of poverty that you yourself experienced: the imitation of Jesus Christ and sharing with the poor.

Returning to Cardinal Garrone, I would like to quote several lines from his book *Poor in Spirit,* which he dedicated to you, in honor of the ideal that you wished to live and your Little Sisters wish to live now: "Little Sisters, poverty is your glory. You work so that, for others, poverty may not be suffering, or at least not fruitless, unrewarding suffering. And you do this at the cost of being poor yourselves, like the Lord Jesus who 'became poor to enrich us by his poverty' (2 Cor 8:9)" (*Poor in Spirit*, p. 9).

— *O! Holy Poverty ... I recommended to the novices, **Poverty, love her well for she will keep you always as good Little Sisters, for the Good God himself loves poverty and blesses those who live by it.***

— Yes, this poverty, which is not a hardship to which you subjected yourself begrudgingly, but one you chose to live in all confidence, is not a speciality of nuns or priests who have made a vow of poverty. All Christians, priests and the laity are called upon by Jesus to follow in his footsteps: "Any of you who does not give up everything he has cannot be my disciple" (Lk 14:33). The Blessed Father de Foucauld said, "The measure of imitation is love." The more we love Jesus, the more we try to imitate him, and the more we, like him, love the poor.

Lord Jesus, give us hearts like the poor!

Reflection Questions

Am I too caught up in the things of this world to give God space in my life? Do I recoil at the idea of being poor? Do I avoid associating with those who are poor or unattractive? Do I understand the difference between giving something to a good cause and really sharing my life and myself with others? How is it possible to give much, even when we don't seem to have much to give? Can I imagine choosing poverty — and actually loving it — because Jesus chose it and loved it?

5
To Depend on God for Everything

Focus Point

Today's reflection brings us full circle on poverty — it *is* beautiful to be poor when we await all from God with complete confidence that he will provide for our needs. Those who truly believe take nothing for granted, but they *know* with an inner certitude that Providence will provide, because God will never abandon the poor. It is actually very simple — to say "I believe in God, the Father almighty" means believing that God truly is almighty, and that he really is a Father who watches over us, his children. Lord, help us to live the Beatitudes with joyful confidence in your Providence.

"It is good to be poor, to have nothing, to depend on God for everything."

"It's true, it's incredible, but if God is with us, it will be accomplished."

"Providence will never fail me."

— My Sister, you chose to be poor and this poverty is an expression of your complete faith in divine Providence. Can you explain this to us, dear Sister?

*— Providence is for us a little like a visitor who announces himself in advance so you know he is coming. Providence does not have to announce itself, yet one is certain that it will come and intervene in our daily lives the moment we are in need. **I know that Providence will never fail me**.*

— How do you know?

*— Because the Lord said that I can count on his word. Did he not say to his disciples, "So do not worry, saying, 'What shall we eat?' or 'What shall we drink?' or 'What shall we wear?' … your heavenly Father knows that you need them" (Mt 6:31–32). Besides, in the **Our Father**, we ask him to give us our daily bread. Having complete faith in the word of the Lord is not a wager but a guarantee. **God will never abandon the poor**.*

— Acting in such a way, my Sister, means having the confidence of a child in his father. This depends on the degree of our faith. The deeper our faith, the more unconditional our confidence in God. Undertaking the establishment of homes for the poor, as you did, without a penny in your pocket and little means to support yourself, has been called foolish by some people.

*— Yes, people said that to me — the authorities, sometimes even my benefactors — but I always told them **if God is with us, it will be accomplished.***

— The beauty of this is that it depends completely on faith. Centuries ago, St. Paul already exclaimed, "But God chose the foolish things of the world to shame the wise" (1 Cor 1:27). And Mr. Dupont, in his enthusiasm at receiving "the Mother of the Little Sisters" shortly after the founding of the home at Tours (1847), said, "The ignorant people of the world believe that this **bread-seeker**, as she called herself, was asking them for alms, but if they opened their eyes, they understood that they themselves would receive by listening to her speak so lovingly and simply of the Providence of God."

Allow me to continue leafing through your archives. Your admirable disciple, Father Ernest Lelièvre, traveled the world establishing and organizing new foundations. When one of your homes was being built in London (1862), afraid of all the bills, he wrote, "I can no longer sleep, or rather I am sleeping on the pillow of my faith in God." He added, "Losing faith would mean that I would have lost my vocation and my memory. God would not let that happen!" Another time, he confided, "I cannot describe the total confidence in Providence that I have had in the past few days."

Beyond the foundations, this total confidence helps us through the days when we rely on Providence for our daily bread. The history of your homes is full of *fioretti* and is a magnificent illustration of this faith. The Little Sisters find it quite normal that Providence plays a natural role in their lives. In this vein, in the beginnings of the house at Rennes (1846), the Mother Superior said, "One evening, the Sister in the kitchen asked me if she should ring the bell for dinner since she had nothing to serve to the Sisters. 'Have the poor had enough to eat?' I asked, to which she answered, 'Yes, dear Mother.' 'Good,' I said, 'You told me too late; now it's supper time and we should ring for dinner as usual.' We went to the refectory. After saying grace, there was a knock at the door. It was a servant carrying a fully prepared meal. We lacked nothing. The Sister came in trembling with excitement at how quickly Providence had come to our aid."

— *It's true what you say:* ***we were very poor, but we were happy.*** *Without counting our efforts, our work and our collections, we did everything we could to meet the needs of our poor. But total confidence in Providence delivered us from worry.*

— At the end of December 1865, Father Lelièvre described the departure of five Little Sisters for Yorkshire "with the usual faith." He admired their Superior, saying, "I have never seen anyone abandon herself so fully to Providence ... By going there, she cherishes Bethlehem. I think that lying on her bed of straw on bare boards, she must hear the angels singing. In this Christmas season, it is highly possible."

Father Lelièvre's life was dedicated to theology. His thesis was rooted in his experience, as he explained, "I am going to write a dissertation (doctorate in theology) and prove it with the story of the Little Sisters of the Poor; the thesis is that one must believe in Almighty God the Father, that he is the all powerful father." Severeal years later, he noted in one of his letters from Edinburgh, "For ten years now I have had the honor of ministering to the Little Sisters. I have seen much in our homes ... The work is like a miracle."

— *My dear Brother, when one has nothing to begin with and one admires the result, the disproportion between poverty and the result makes it perfectly clear that it is God who was responsible for everything.*

— One who abandons himself to divine Providence resembles someone who throws himself into the water with his eyes closed, with total acceptance of the fact that he will no longer have "terra firma" under his feet. "The heart of poverty is the fact of 'casting oneself' on the Lord ... and of consenting to our life's being uniquely dependent on him ... in trusting him to support us, in refusing to rely on material things for the props that they are naturally supposed to afford us" (*Poor in Spirit,* pp. 26–27). What one may call "a leap of faith" places our safety in God. Sister Jeanne of Cancale, your words would be much like those of Sister Thérèse of Lisieux, who was six years old when you died. She wrote, "Depend on the Good Lord for everything as a child depends on his father for everything … don't worry about anything." Preaching this may not seem reasonable to some!

— *But, dear Father, is it possible to be reasonable if one follows the Gospel as a rule of conduct?*

*Allow me to tell you about something that happened towards the end of my life. I sometimes received visits from important people, people who were full of faith and charity, like viscount Coëtlosquet. I didn't think too long about what to say to them: **I spoke to them of Providence.** It is Providence that counts; **I wasn't considered to be much on earth.** Perhaps you have read that a few years before my death, the municipality of Saint-Servan wanted to give my name to the street where our first old people's home was located. When I heard of this decision, I was very upset, so I hurried to see Father Collet, the Vicar of Saint-Servan, to beg him to intervene with the municipality and ask them to call the street Providence Street. Unfortunately, this wasn't possible.*

— It is true that faith in Providence plays an important role in the daily lives of the Little Sisters.

— So that our confidence is based on faith, and that our Sisters count on Providence rather than being tempted to rely on reserves of money, I have always insisted that "the Little Sisters have no dowry or revenues," meaning that they "cannot receive any private income or have a fixed income or trust fund." In 1865, after twenty-five years of existence, our Congregation was well known and could have benefited from financial support from a growing number of legacies that were being made on the condition that they be converted into allowances. The Sisters asked themselves if they should embark on this path of security. Before the General Council, I defended the spirit of our work, which since its origins had never relied on human means but had put all its faith in God. A letter to the Minister of Justice appended with our signatures confirmed this viewpoint, "It is contrary to the spirit of the community and its rule of life to accept fixed income and revenues such as allowances from the state."

— You must have been very happy to see this choice of poverty assured for the future.

— Of course, and later, when I was 86 years old, to my great joy, I learned that on March 1, 1879, Pope Leo XIII approved the Constitutions of the Congregation. The Little Sisters could continue to live in poverty, in the same way as they had always done.

— Dear Sister, I understand and admire the fact that you defended your ideals. But in practical terms, how can we abandon ourselves to divine Providence? It is not an excuse for nonchalance or laziness? When we undertake a project, we invest everything of ourselves and pray with insistence, but we must also put our trust in God. Evangelical wisdom contradicts human prudence and may render the Christian position uncomfortable. When one looks to a future, secured by guarantees, insurance, and precautionary measures, is it possible to leave room for divine Providence? Can it answer the call of the unforeseeable?

In keeping with the Beatitudes, one must live from day to day with joyful trust in our heavenly Father!

Reflection Questions

Jesus said, "Do not fear ... your heavenly Father knows what you need." Am I afraid? What do I fear? What is keeping me from trusting *completely* in God and his loving Providence? Do I really understand that my life is entirely dependent on God? Or do I pride myself, rather, in thinking that I am independent? Have I ever had to cast myself on the Lord, because I had no support other than him? Could the memory of such an experience help me to deepen my faith and confidence in God? Can I imagine ever saying that "we were poor but happy?"

6
Only the Little Are Pleasing to God

Focus Point

///////////

Our society teaches us that if we are to count, to get ahead in life, we must impose ourselves, dominate others, find some way of standing out in the crowd. But Jesus tells us that just the opposite is true: "Whoever wishes to be great must be the least of all and the servant of all." It is a matter of following Our Lord, who humbled himself for us. It is not a question of pretending, but of realizing that we really are small, insignificant and weak creatures before God. Only through littleness can we realize our greatness — that of being children of God, uniquely dependent on him.

///////////

"You must be little before the Good Lord. When you pray, start like this ... stand before the Good God as a little frog."

"We must be very little and very humble, to believe ourselves to be the least. O! If we come to believe ourselves to be something, to wish to appear to be great, the Congregation will no longer be blessed by the good God and that will be our downfall."

"You must allow yourself to be humiliated. Instead of turning in on yourself, you must turn towards God."

— In the Gospel, Jesus calls a child and places him among his disciples, saying to them, "I tell you truly, unless you change and become like little children, you will never enter the Kingdom of Heaven" (Mt 18:3). Your institute, my Sister, was known as the Servants and Sisters of the Poor until 1849, in Nantes, when you added *Little*, giving it its final name of the Little Sisters of the Poor, about which a chronicler wrote, "Popular wisdom found the correct term … the word seemed a good fit and the association adopted it." Throughout the world, it now symbolizes what you wanted it to. Was it not enough to be a servant and sister of the poor? What meaning does *Little* add?

— *First of all, you must understand that my companions and I were largely poor, uneducated girls from the countryside. We were not society ladies and didn't dream of becoming so by becoming nuns. We lived and spent our time with the poor. Undoubtedly, it is because of this that people who knew us called us the "little sisters."*

— My Sister, you kept telling the novices, **"Little, be very little! If you become great, our Congregation will fall."** What exactly did you mean by this?

— *Being little is obviously the opposite of being great. Moreover, the Word of God that you just cited answers the disciples' question, "Who is the greatest in the Kingdom of Heaven?"*

*Referring to the little child, Jesus affirms the exact opposite of what one is used to believing: "He who makes himself as small as a child is the greatest in the Kingdom of Heaven." Being great implies wanting to impose oneself, to dominate; it means wanting to shine, to be appreciated, to believe oneself to be some-thing. Jesus explained this well to the Apostles with the story of Zebedee's sons, whose mother asked for first place in the Kingdom of Heaven. Jesus answered, "You know that the rulers of the Gentiles lord it over them … It must not be so with you. Instead, who-ever wants to become great among you must be your servant" (Mt 20:25–26). This is why we wanted to become the servants of the poor; this means greatness in the eyes of Jesus. When I became a religious, those who had known "the tall Jeanne" asked me what they should call me. I just wanted to **be the humble servant of the poor**.*

— So at heart, being little is closely related to humility?

— *That's right. For twenty years, every morning, we recited St. John Eudes's prayer of humility: "Lord*

Jesus Christ, I am nothing; I can do nothing … I am the least of all." It seems normal for us to say to the Lord, "I am nothing," because Jesus himself assured us, "Apart from me you can do nothing" (Jn 15:5). Humility is more difficult when it comes to others — being little in relation to others. We must accept being humiliated **by following the example of Our Lord, who humbled himself for us.** *In community life, in our relations with others, in our collecting and* **with our masters the poor,** *there are so many opportunities for us to be humble and little.*

— It seems that you often insisted that the Little Sisters and postulants walk quietly and close the doors and windows softly. Why did you attach such importance to such details?

— *When one is quiet, one passes unnoticed — this is a way of being little. Moreover, I believe that* **Our Lord dislikes a lot of noise, and we must consider that he is in our presence.** *In the early days of our work, we used to make ourselves very little. At night, when Anne and Isabelle had gone to sleep, so as not to disturb them and to favor our meditation, we took off our shoes to climb up to the attic to say our prayers …*

— A few years later, a visitor at your home in Dinan says that he was surprised to see you and your Sisters squatting on your heels singing hymns. Am I right in thinking that this position inspired you to compare yourselves to little frogs?

— *I'm not sure. In our first years, our houses were very poorly furnished. We lacked many things, including chairs. The elderly used the ones we did have, so we Sisters did without. That's why we got into the habit of sitting back on our heels. What is important in my comparison is not holding oneself as a little frog before God, but simply to **be little before God**. Just because one has a certain authority does not mean that we have to stop being little: **when one is in charge (of a responsibility), if one does not remain little, it is like stealing from the Good Lord.***

— As you say, my dear Sister, humility keeps us in our place before God.

— *Of course, because **we must behave as we truly are — poor, weak, and incapable of any good**. I know it is difficult to believe, but God can help us achieve such an interior attitude. In the years before the war (after 1870), I often walked in the garden of the novitiate, with my little stick in one hand and my rosary in the other. During recreation, I met with the many nuns and we admired the wild roses together, which actually allowed me to make a little comparison: **You see these rose bushes? They are growing wild. You too are growing wild, but if you allow yourself to be well formed, you will become a beautiful rose, fashioned by the love of God; but you must allow yourself to be humiliated. Instead of turning in on yourself, you must turn towards God.***

— How difficult it is to become humble! I think our training in this respect never ends. Our spiritual leaders, neighbors, and life's events act as intermediaries in this process, but it is God who takes care of our training.

— We are always novices! *If you want to be a good religious, remember often your novitiate; But especially, no matter what age you are, always consider yourself a novice and you will see that all will go well for you.*

— It is not only religious who must continue to train themselves regardless of age. It is very dangerous in our spiritual life to believe that one can no longer change, that there is nothing more to learn. When we feel we have lost our enthusiasm, we resemble old wine skins, blaming the Lord that they are no longer able to hold new wine.

We are then called to become like children again. All of us hear this imperative of the Lord. He explains to Nicodemus that even if one is old in body, one can be born again in the spirit (Jn 3:4–8). Spiritual childhood does not mean childishness. Humility is at its root, as well as spiritual poverty, which renounces all possessions in order to receive all from God. "We tend to think of a loss or a diminution. But in fact, by virtue of this loss, the soul aligns herself precisely on God, she mounts towards him, she lightens herself to rise" (*Poor in Spirit,* p. 74). The soul's littleness imparts her with invisible greatness: "The soul is aware of growing greater, but only in the sense that she feels the love of God growing within her; and thus, she 'dilates,' if we may use the word, though human eyes cannot see the change" (*ibid.*).

— *What you just cited is profoundly true. Littleness does not diminish us but transforms us.*

I don't know how many times I repeated to the novices what has almost become my legacy: *"My little ones, make the most of your novitiate and refuse God nothing. Above all, learn to be humble, and when you are in the homes, be very little. If you keep the spirit of humility and simplicity, never seeking the world's esteem, then God will be glorified and you will obtain the conversion of souls. If you become big and proud, the Congregation will fall."*

Reflection Questions

Where do I place more energy — into building myself up in the eyes of others, or into growing closer to God, as his beloved child? Am I always trying to get ahead? Am I overly competitive? Am I willing to recognize the gifts and talents of others, and to let them shine? What is more important — that I be recognized, or that God be glorified?

7
Ring in God's Name and God Will Bless Us

Focus Point

///////////

To embrace poverty out of love for the one who made himself poor for our sake ... to share our lives with the poor ... to count on God to provide all that is lacking. This is what Jeanne Jugan challenges us to through the example of her life. Among the rich she made herself a spokesperson for the poor. She gave prophetic witness that as children of God, we are all brothers and sisters, called to share the goods of creation and to care for one another. It is a question of recognizing our radical solidarity as God's creatures, of living the Beatitudes in the concrete realities of daily life. Lord, give us hearts that are humble and poor, hearts that are open to give and to receive.

///////////

" I went out collecting with my basket for our poor; this cost me, but I did it for God and our dear poor people."

Seizing the rope of the bell:

"Don't worry if you're badly received. Ring for the Lord and he will bless us."

"You will go collecting and people will send you away with unkind words. But you must never show your dissatisfaction because, you see my little ones, when you are badly received, it is good for you: you can offer it up to the Good Lord."

— The collecting, my dear Sister, took up a large part of your life and continues to be an important part of the lives of the Little Sisters today.

— *When I left one family, for whom I had worked as a servant, explaining that I was going to collect for the elderly poor wandering the city, Mr. Leroy exclaimed, "You're mad, my poor Jeanne, you don't have a penny to your name. How are you going to feed yourself?" Spontaneously, but with deep conviction I answered,* **"I will go out collecting and no one will refuse me bread for the elderly poor for whom I feel such great compassion; God will help me."**

— The number of people you welcomed did not stop growing. Only one month after you had moved into the "big basement" (1841), your new home was full: twelve elderly women had found shelter with you. One wonders how you fed these women, who were "broken by the years and infirmity" and no longer able to appeal to their benefactors. Well, you simply decided to take their place and go begging for them instead. You changed roles — not content just to welcome the poor, you became poor yourself, collecting alms, sometimes being the one to give, sometimes the one who received. Receiving everything from others was synonymous with receiving everything from God. Divested of everything you owned, you prepared yourself for this spiritual poverty of which you spoke, recommending us to "depend on God for everything." We understand why religious are asked to be materially poor, this way the spiritual is not something disembodied.

Time and time again, you walked the streets with your big basket on your arm, "a basket known all over town," collecting alms from charitable people "who had habitually helped the poor people staying with you, since they were now unable to go knocking on their benefactors' doors themselves." They also gave you the "leftovers from their meals, old linen and clothes they no longer wore." Sometimes you had a lot to carry and you were tired, yet you still carried home everything you could to your "masters, the poor." You took their place and became a beggar yourself.

— *Like a little **servant of the poor**.*

— In the introduction to the Constitutions of 1852, it is written that "to feed the poor well and answer their needs," you and your companions "felt the pressing need to gather for your poor people and in their name what the rich didn't need, their old furniture and the crumbs from their table." Your actions set the tone in the city for a "large human family, in which all men are brothers and are invited to share the goods of creation" (*Constitutions,* 107). Creating a great sense of solidarity, you were the spokesperson of the poor among the rich. St. Paul asked that, through the collecting, the surplus of some provide for the others' needs (2 Cor 8:14). It is true that the solution to the problem of misery surpasses the possibilities of personal charity, so people must work together to create an institution such as yours. In this way, charity becomes collective, less personal, but more effective.

— *You know, dear Brother, I did not invent the collecting; it was a tradition in Cancale. Collections for neighbors without work or for widows were frequent. We were just two women who took the initiative to go from door to door with a bag that people filled with coins big and small. We also had the example of St. John of God, who, having established his hospital in Grenada, went to the city asking for alms and medicine. The Brothers of St. John of God taught us how to proceed.*

— When you were unjustly removed from your responsibility as Superior of your Congregation, you dedicated yourself for many years to the task of begging for alms.

— For me, I was the little beggar. I asked, I held out my hand, and our kind benefactors gave to the Lord's poor ones.

— Your experience allowed you to guide your younger Sisters who were sent out begging.

— Yes, of course. I especially insisted that we show the utmost respect and sensitivity towards those we approached; no one was to feel obliged to give to us. I told the novices to **be careful not to rush when asking for charity and not to ask straightaway for what you need ... as if they owed it to you to give. But take the time to greet them, and if the opportunity arises, take interest in the people and events of the moment ... It is more humble and less hurried ... Then you can gently tell them, without persistence, of the needs of your home.**

— After everything I have read, it seems to me, my Sister, that begging for alms is a hard way of learning about life. Moreover, the Constitutions explain that begging for alms "necessitates an attitude of humility and interior poverty and makes us live the spirit of the Beatitudes without illusion. It bears witness to our confidence in God, which makes us rely on the intervention of Providence, without however neglecting human means" (*Constitutions*, 108). Begging for alms indeed requires great humility, especially when one is not welcome …

— *Some refusals were even insulting. It isn't easy to accept this and remain calm and polite. Sometimes I was treated like an idler. People said things like, "Why don't you get a job?" to which I replied, "This is for my poor, Sir." When I was shown the door, I always said, "**Thank you**!" Some thought me mad to thank them for throwing me out, but all the same, my final words were, "**It's for the Good Lord.**"*

— Have you not been reproached for turning your poor into people who receive handouts and do nothing in exchange for everything they receive?

— *From the beginning, they put themselves to work, carrying out household tasks or helping with construction, cultivating the garden, carding wool, sewing, and knitting, and performing many other tasks. Sometimes I would go into town with my basket full of knitted sweaters, handkerchiefs and other objects they had made for me to sell. Everyone was busy all day and did what they could to the best of their abilities. And they prayed with us each day for our benefactors.*

— The experience of the Brothers of St. John of God helped you. Less than twenty years before your first collections, their Provincial recommended his brothers to "take delight in being spurned or when you are badly received. Do not argue with anyone; it is an occasion for you to grow. Never speak badly of anyone. Say that you are happy with everyone when you are asked about those who receive you badly ..." (P. Magallon, 1825). Your advice, my Sister, was brimming with the same evangelic zeal when you said to your little "bread-seekers," *"When the neighbors say, 'I'm sure you didn't receive a warm welcome next door,' never let your dissatisfaction show. In such cases, I simply said, 'Well, those people were good to me.' You see, my little ones, when you are received poorly, it is good for you and gives you something to offer up to God."*

So, what you are saying is that not only must we refuse to speak ill of anyone but we must also refrain from encouraging idle gossip in others, by offering them nothing bad to say about each other. The latter is certainly harder to achieve since conversations often lead beyond where we intended them to go. A heart full of goodness, however, will not allow itself to be taken by surprise.

Do we not tend to look critically on those who take us by the hand? Or do we not condemn those who do not assist people in distress, with the good conscience of the Pharisee? When the Lord declares, "Do not judge, or you too will be judged," he foresees no exceptions. What follows should make us shudder: "For in the same

way you judge others, you will be judged, and
with the measure you use, it will be measured to
you" (Mt 7:1–2). Let us make this our maxim:
Be too good to be sure you are good enough!

Reflection Questions

As I grow closer to God, am I also drawn
closer to my brothers and sisters in Christ? Am
I open to seeing their needs and to sharing with
them? Do I really understand that if I claim
to love God, I must also love my brothers and
sisters, and that this has practical implications?
Am I ashamed or embarrassed to be identified
with the poor, the unpopular? Or do I dare to
share something of myself with them — the
best of myself, just as Jesus gave his life for
those whom the world despised?

8

Jesus Is Waiting
for You in the Chapel

Focus Point

////////////

Jesus promised to come and dwell in the hearts
of those who love him and keep his word (cf. Jn
14:23). Jeanne Jugan was aware of the living presence of Christ within her, in the tabernacle and in
the poor. Her confidence in Providence extended
to her spiritual life, for when she spoke to Jesus
present in the Blessed Sacrament, she spoke to him
as a friend. She knew that he would really hear her
and that he would take care of everything, "for he
has a good memory." Lord, help us to remember
that you are waiting for us in the tabernacle, in the
poor and in our own souls.

////////////

*"The Good God is our Father. Let us place
ourselves in his hands."*

"When your strength and patience are giving out, when you feel lonely and helpless, say to him: 'You know well what is happening, my dear Jesus. I have only you ...' And then go your way and don't worry. It is enough to have told our good Lord. He has an excellent memory."

— The Sisters say that you had great respect for the Rule of Life of the Little Sisters. When they were novices, you made them pray "to have more and more love for the practice of the Rule." Of course, you also made them pray for the Pope, the Congregation, the Superiors, and "for the Little Sisters, in particular for those who suffer or are tempted."

— *I did not want to limit myself to the needs of the Congregation. I was anxious to open our minds and our hearts to all of the intentions that represented the needs of our time, like the harvest and the harvesters, the soldiers and those injured during the war (1870), the safety of the workers who were constructing the new buildings of La Tour Saint-Joseph, not to mention those in the mission countries who did not know Christ.*

— My Sister, in your prayers, did you address the Good God or Jesus?

— *When I was reminding the Sisters of the **triple presence of God** — in us, in the tabernacle, and in the poor, it is clear that I was referring to Our*

Lord Jesus Christ. **The poor are the suffering members of Our Lord.** *It is he who is present in us, and our reverence is inspired by his presence. Moreover, I meditated on the works of Father Nouet, who asks us to place ourselves in the "School of Jesus."*

— On reading Father Nouet, you found a sense of family in the spirituality of St. John Eudes which was deeply marked by the French school of the 17th century, inspired by Cardinal de Bérulle.

— *I learned that Jesus is present in us and that his presence carries that of the Holy Trinity: "If anyone loves me, he will obey my teaching. My Father will love him, and we will come to him and make our home with him" (Jn 14:23).*

— You agree with what Father Peyriguère wrote: "Christ is in you ... It is no longer you who are living, but Christ who is living in you. It is not you who are praying, it is not you who are acting, but Christ who is praying in you, and it is Christ who is acting in you. He never leaves you, not for a single moment."[1] In these lines, he is doing nothing but making explicit the words of St. Paul: "I no longer live, but Christ lives in me" (Gal 2:20).

Jesus Christ is in us, not as an object but as a living being, in order to be the inspiration for our behavior in our daily lives, so that our words are the words of Jesus who lives in us, and that our actions are those of Jesus acting in us and through us. In this way, whether we are peeling potatoes or are immersed in mystical theological texts, everything is important since Christ lives in us, and it is through him that our actions are Christlike and acquire infinite significance. You say, *"Nothing is small, everything is great. You must do everything with love ..."*

— *And if it is painful, we must say to ourselves* ***it is for Jesus.***

— My Sister, you also met Jesus in the Eucharist, and received Communion as often as was permitted.

— *On the evenings before Communion, after the Benediction of the Blessed Sacrament, I sang a little song to the novices, "Oh my dear Jesus, my soul desires you, etc.," and made dramatic gestures towards the tabernacle.*

At Mass, the priest recited the Our Father alone, and I urged the Little Sisters to say it with him. How effective these requests of the Our Father are when they are united in this way with those of Our Lord, whose place the priest takes! ***And Jesus, he is really there on the altar and will grant us all that we ask of him.*** *He is there for us ...*

I really enjoyed the Feast of Corpus Christi and the procession in the garden with the altar of repose. It was magnificent! And at night, when I couldn't sleep, I united with Masses celebrated in faraway countries.

— In your final years, you went from the infirmary to the tribune of the chapel, spending hours in adoration of the Blessed Sacrament, as Father de Foucauld would do twenty years later. I believe that you spoke to Our Lord like a friend. You undoubtedly said to him, *"You know what is happening, my Good Jesus. You know everything."* You must have suffered terribly having been unjustly relegated, under used, humiliated too often, and misjudged by the younger Sisters, from whom the truth about your role in the founding of the Congregation had been hidden. Only Jesus knew how much you had gone through, and you said to him, *"I only have you and you know everything."*

Through your long humiliation, in your lifetime, it was as though you were dead, but what some did not realize was that you were like a grain of wheat that lies dormant in the soil, only to bear fruit. Yet one admired the harvest, not knowing what part you had invisibly played. Do you remember the hundreds of postulants that joyously surrounded you on the Feast of St. Joseph in 1867?

Kneeling before the Blessed Sacrament, you conversed with Jesus and spent hours in silent adoration. For when we enter the chapel to adore him, it is not because we need him, but because he is present and waiting for us. First and foremost, in our praise, we recognize him for who he is. He is the Word of God, he who gave his life for us. Our visit is unselfish since we go to see him because we love him, simply and gratuitously. Perhaps we prostrate ourselves before him or pray with the aid of the Gospel, in which we find him. And we keep telling him that we love him even when we don't feel anything.

Lord Jesus, let our faith grow! May we allow you to live in us! May you find us transparent!

Your are present in our brothers and in the Blessed Sacrament where you present yourself to us, but it is not because you are infinitely patient that we may allow ourselves to make you wait!

Reflection Questions

How aware am I of Jesus' presence in my soul? Do I take time to talk with him, as one would talk to a friend? Do I see my life as a continuation of his? What do these words of St. Paul mean to me, "It is no longer I who live, for Christ lives in me"? Am I also aware of Christ's presence in the Eucharist? Do I attend Mass regularly? Do I participate actively? Do I take time out from my busy schedule to visit him in the Blessed Sacrament, to spend time with him as one spends time with a friend? Has Jesus been waiting a long time to see me?

9
We Must Always Say: Blessed Be God

Focus Point

///////////

The way we approach life is up to each one of us. It can be hard to praise God when things are not going our way, when our faith in him, and our confidence in his Providence, are tested. But that's just what Jeanne Jugan did. Her habitual response to life's events was "Blessed be God ... thank you, my God ... glory be to God!" She repeated this refrain in sunshine and in rain (and there are a lot of rainy days in Brittany), in good times and bad. She was like Job, who said, "The Lord gave and the Lord has taken away; blessed be the name of the Lord!" What was Jeanne's secret? Intimacy with God. She saw in each event a manifestation of God's loving plan for her, and she glorified him by embracing his will — by fulfilling his plan for her — joyfully. Lord, give us faith to see your loving Providence in all things, and give us grateful hearts ready to thank you.

//////////////

"In our joys, in our troubles, when we are treated with disdain, we must always say: Thank you God! Glory be to God!"

"In all things, everywhere, in all circumstances, I say over and over again, Blessed be God!"

— Since 1852, you were obliged to stop your collecting rounds and your other activities in the Congregation, and remain cloistered in the shadows and silence of the Motherhouse until your death. No one knows what you felt during these twenty-seven years. I imagine it couldn't have been easy to subdue a sentiment of revolt and not to show your pain. You nevertheless kept on smiling and praising God.

— *I know that in the face of adversity, one should throw oneself into the arms of Our Lord Jesus, who said, "Come to me, all you who are weary and burdened, and I will give you rest" (Mt 11:28). In the secret of prayer, we can speak freely with God as did the holy man Job, who is a model of resignation for us, and Jesus in Gethesmane, who asked his Father to remove the cup from him before accepting "that his will be done." St. Paul claimed that we would not be tempted beyond what we can bear: "No temptation has seized you except what is common to man. And God is faithful ... But when you are tempted, he will also provide a way out so that you can stand up under it" (1 Cor 10:13). Every day in the Our Father, we ask God to give us the grace not to be led into temptation. So in prayer, with his grace, we find the peace of acceptance and can* **continue to say "Thank you my Lord, or Glory be to God!"**

— Popular wisdom recommends that we make the best of every situation. In fact, it seems quite unreasonable to grumble about or rebel against what we cannot change, whether it be bad weather or a broken leg!

— *I remember one year at La Tour during haymaking season, it was raining very heavily. The novices were filled with dismay, so to bring a smile to their faces, I said,* **"Always keep smiling. Blessed be God! Blessed be God!"**

— That reminds me of something an elderly woman I was visiting said during terrible wind and rain. I said to her, "What awful weather!" and she replied maliciously, "What do you want Father! It's God's weather ... but it's not his most beautiful!" She wasn't well educated, but she had a sense of humor that gave her the grace to accept things the way they were and take life in stride.

— *Thousands of times a day and* **in all circumstances, I say Blessed be God!**

— The verb *bless* and the adjective *blessed*, although used liberally in the Bible, are hardly used in today's everyday language, perhaps because they are no longer well understood. Could one not explain the benediction of God by saying that God is content with us and is expressing his benevolence, or is wishing us well. It's very simple.

With the heart of a child, we ask God to bless our loved ones and our actions, to bless our table or the family gathered around it for a meal, or to bless a journey we will take by car or plane. Yet how can we poor mortals bless God who is "above all blessing and praise?" (Neh 9:5). Following your example, my Sister, we nevertheless allow ourselves to bless God.

This means, regardless of our situation, whether pleasant or painful, we are pleased with God and give him thanks. Rain or shine, in sickness or in health, we are pleased with God despite everything, and bless him, singing, "Blessed be God in all and forever!" Whatever happens, blessing him, thanking him, and glorifying him is our duty. St. Paul declared that there is no excuse if in knowing God, "they neither glorified him as God nor gave thanks to him" (Rm 1:21).

— *We bless God and give him thanks more spontaneously so that good things might happen to us. With a joyful heart, I thanked Divine Providence for*

*the many postulants who came to La Tour from far
and wide and for the teams of novices working indus-
triously in the farms. We must be eternally grateful
to those who help us. Every day I had prayers said
for our benefactors. It is Divine Providence that sends
them to us: never forget to thank him or Our Lady.*

— Always give thanks. Allow me to cite
Léon Aubineau, who confirms your message,
"Is to thank not the secret of being able to
obtain? And if Jeanne thanked and wanted us
to thank, how much more did she thank Divine
Providence?" (1883). But to thank God in suffering, it is only faith that can help us overcome
our natural reactions. You say again and again,
"We must suffer joyfully." Admittedly, many
who read your words would like to know the
secret of such joy.

— *It all depends on how intimate we are with
Jesus.*

— Yet confronted with the death of those we
love, God does not stop us from shedding tears
or from suffering terribly from loss. St. Paul only
asks us to suffer and cry differently from those
who have no hope: "Brothers, we do not want
you to … grieve like the rest of men, who have
no hope. We believe that Jesus died and rose
again and so we believe that God will bring
with Jesus those who have fallen asleep in him"
(1 Th 4:13–14).

— When one of the Sisters died, I noticed that the other sisters and novices were sad, but I asked them to embrace the day of the funeral with joy. **God be praised! It is a day of joy. Here is one that has gone to paradise, entering into glory. Our turn will come soon enough and we must prepare ourselves.**

— You talk of entering into glory. The word *glory* is not common today, except for in our history books, which tell of the armed struggles of generals who were covered in glory. But how can the glory of God be explained? Can it be described as the success of God? If, in our liberty, we do not place any obstacle before him, God will succeed in what he dreams for us. He is proud of us: "Lord Jesus may be glorified in you, and you in him" (2 Th 1:12).

Elizabeth of the Trinity, whom I greatly admire, wanted to be for God the "praise of glory," fulfilling the ideal proposed by St. Paul: "In him we were also chosen, having been predestined according to the plan of him who works out everything in conformity with the purpose of his will, in order that we, who were the first to hope in Christ, might be for the praise of his glory" (Eph 1:11–12). Since the Vatican Council II, we can use the fourth Eucharistic Prayer, which takes up the same theme: "Through the power of the Holy Spirit, gather all who worthily share in this Holy Sacrament into the one body of Christ, as a living sacrifice of praise."

10
Do Everything through Love

Focus Point

//////////////

St. John wrote, "We must love because he first loved us" (1 Jn 4:19). The Christian life is so simple — we must do everything through love in response to Christ's love for us. This love is revealed to us in Jesus' self-emptying to become a man, in his Passion and in his Sacred Heart. It is revealed to us in a totally unique way in the Eucharist — Jesus' ultimate gift to us on the altar — where he gives us his very body and blood. Heart of Jesus, help us to follow you along the way of love, to give back love for love.

//////////////

"Refuse God nothing ... We must do everything through love."

"All for you, my Jesus."

"Allow yourself to be formed by the Good God and you will become a beautiful rose of charity."

"Love God very much."

— Following the Gospel and the Saints, you said that the poor are Our Lord Jesus; it is he whom we welcome and care for in them. Yet, sometimes we might find a person particularly difficult, and any amount of patience cannot seem to make that person understand what might be good for him or her ... Of course, Jesus is not unpleasant, yet the person we are dealing with happens to be unbearable ...

— The Good God asks us to overcome our imme-diate reactions so that our love can grow stronger. For me, this is not a question of duty but of love. In instances where we are not naturally drawn to someone, it is charity which guides our willingness to act. Our good disposition does not always suffice: we must prepare ourselves through prayer. I told the novices, ***"Come, let us pray. You must not pray just for prayer's sake, but you have need of a great deal of grace to become good Little Sisters."***

— When you insisted that we must *love God very much*, "On your lips, each of these affirma-tions is alive, already lived, taken as they stand, the bearer of a conviction rooted in the depths of your being" (*Sayings of Jeanne Jugan*, p. 63). The Constitutions of the Little Sisters lay down

that "We will make charity the soul of our conduct" (*Constitutions,* 78), not obedience to a rule,
nor an obligation, but charity. If this is true for
the Little Sisters, then surely this should apply
to all Christians in their relations with others.
Every event and person in our lives represents
an opportunity for us to transcend ourselves.
In this way, even if abnegation is required, our
heart will gradually become one that knows
how to love. You compared this long appren-
ticeship to the work of a stonemason.

— *The construction of the chapel at La Tour
inspired me to make this comparison. I could see the
workers from the window, and I said to the novices,
**"Look at these workers cutting this white stone,
making it into something beautiful: You must let
yourself be formed by Our Lord in the same way."**
Clearly, I was thinking of their formation in the
religious life, of all that is required by obedience to
the Rule, to the Sisters responsible for the novices and
to our Superiors, placing great love in this obedience
which is sometimes quite mortifying. **Allow yourself
to be formed by the Good God and you will become
a beautiful rose of charity.***

— We are also in the novitiate of life. Our
masters of novices are the events, big and small,
that we experience every day. As Pascal said,
"If God gives us masters in his name. Oh! We
must obey them with all our heart! Necessity
and events require this without fail." The often

unexpected meeting of events and people that may upset or hurt me, oblige me to listen attentively, or demand my patience; make me suffer, or even fill me with joy, constitute not only the school of total confidence in Providence but also the school of love that teaches us that Jesus loves us and that we must love him through everything we experience.

Father Lelièvre, whom we spoke of earlier, took as his motto, "Who will separate us from the charity of Jesus Christ?" and commented, "This is my recipe in all my troubles, the balm for all my ills, the remedy for every pain. Concerns, worries, troubles of the soul, wanderings and phantoms of the imagination, terrors, chronic fears, insomnia, nightmares, confusion, anxiety, dark predictions, depression, political unrest, financial disasters, etc., the cure for all of these is the love of Christ. St. Paul assured us that "nothing will separate us from the love of God that is in Jesus Christ our Lord" (Rm 8:39).

— *Yes, this is exactly what Father Lelièvre preached to the Little Sisters. They used to say that he knew the Gospel of St. Paul by heart! Speaking in this way of the love of God gives me comfort. Formed by St. John Eudes, we had great devotion to the Sacred Heart of Jesus. The Rule of the Third Order required that, for one hour in the morning, we "retreat into the divine heart of Jesus, keeping silence while at work." And we had to recite the Litany of the Sacred Heart every day. I don't know if this is still done today, but these multiple invocations made us sing of God's love for us.*

— In the manner in which Father de Foucauld presents the Sacred Heart, the Crucifix not only raises our hearts but also takes root there. The same Crucifix that Christians contemplate on the walls of houses, by the side of the road, or shining forth from the heart of our churches can only be explained by the love symbolized by the Sacred Heart. It is out of love that Jesus allowed himself to be crucified, out of love for us, for every one of us: "I thought of you in my agony. I shed drops of blood for you," says Pascal for Jesus.

During Mass, in the festive atmosphere of the church, surrounded by flowers, candles, and incense, we are not shocked when we hear the priest declare Jesus's words, "This is my body given for you. This is my blood shed for you." While listening to this, we should imagine the suffering of his Passion and his atrocious death on the cross. Inversely, when I contemplate Jesus, crucified in infinite pain on the cross, I should hear his voice whispering to me, "This is my body given for you. This is my blood shed for you and for all men." In all history, this is surely the most moving declaration of love ever made, especially when I think that these very human words are the words of God. This is my faith; this is our unwavering Christian faith.

On the altar, Jesus's ultimate gift to us — to all of humanity — is made present in the Blessed Sacrament. Although prodigious, it does not stop there. It is his eternally glorious body that is made present, which is perhaps beyond our comprehension of time, but can be explained in that everything happens simultaneously in timeless eternity.

What fantastic direction this gives my daily life! As you say, my Sister, do everything out of love in response to his love. In this regard, St. John wrote, "We love because he first loved us," (1 Jn 4:19) and Thérèse of Lisieux said, "Dear Jesus, I know that love can only be repaid with love."

I say to myself over and over again: He loves me. It is magnificent! A lifelong betrothal! Even when the hour of trial comes — Thérèse of Lisieux, who knew trial, confided that at night, she knew that "above the clouds, his Sun (divine love) is always shining, that its rays are never eclipsed for a moment."

Dear Heart of Jesus, blazing fire of charity, have mercy on us. Dear Heart of Jesus, full of love and kindness, source of consolation, have mercy on us. Dear Heart of Jesus, desired for all eternity, King and heart of hearts, have mercy on us!

Reflection Questions

Doing everything through love requires the strength to overcome our first impressions; this strength is gained through prayer — do I take time out for prayer, especially to participate in the Eucharist, the greatest source of love? Do I know how to draw on these inner reserves of love in my daily life? Is Christ's great love for me a source of inspiration in my daily challenges? Pascal put these words on the lips of Jesus: "I thought of you in my agony." How often do I think of Jesus in his agony? Does this thought spur me on to love? Jeanne Jugan often said, "Refuse God nothing" — what am I holding back from God?

11
It Was God Who Did Everything

Focus Point

////////////

At some point in our spiritual journey, each of us must come to terms with an unsettling truth: we are fundamentally incapable of saving ourselves; alone we are incapable of becoming saints. Far from being discouraged, this realization was a source of profound peace for Jeanne Jugan. As clear-sighted as she was about her own weakness, she was equally confident in God's power and mercy. In this respect she echoes the conviction of St. Paul: "The Lord said to me, 'My grace is sufficient for you, for my power is made perfect in weakness.' Therefore I will boast all the more gladly about my weaknesses, so that Christ's power may rest on me" (2 Cor 12:8–9). Similar sentiments were expressed by St. Thérèse of Lisieux, to whose "little way" Jeanne Jugan's spirituality is often compared: "Holiness is not found in a particular practice but consists of a disposition of the heart which makes us humble and small in the arms of God, conscious of our weakness, and boldly confident in his goodness as our Father." Is this not just another expression of spiritual poverty, which finds it beautiful to be poor, to depend on God for everything? Lord, help us to accept our weakness and increase our confidence in your merciful love.

///////////

"The Good God has been good to me. It is God who has done everything."

"To know how to efface oneself in humility in all that God wants of us, as being only the instruments of his work."

"We would have no more strength against temptation than a little bird against the hawk, were not God to give us his help, and that we should be convinced of this when asking him for it — but this should also increase our trust, since it is by God's power that we can triumph."

— We have spoken much of having total confidence in Providence on a material level. You tell us that *it is good to have nothing and to depend on God for everything*. This attitude must become ours on a spiritual level and in regard to our holiness, which lies beyond our powers.

*— Yes, dear Brother, in moments of temptation
and in the battle against our weaknesses, we must
have **faith in God since it is by God's power that
we can triumph**.*

— In what you say, I hear two "different
movements" inseparable from the path towards
holiness. The Roman centurion in the Gospel
expresses this magnificently, so much so that
we repeat his words at each Mass: "Lord, I do
not deserve to have you come under my roof.
But just say the word, and my servant will
be healed" (Mt 8:8). In the same passage, he
admits his unworthiness and demonstrates his
unquestioning faith in the power of the Lord.
Recognizing our weakness in the face of temptation and failure, without strength or merit, we
become *like the little bird against the hawk*. And
at the same time, we are absolutely convinced
that with *God's power*, we are capable of everything. By accepting that we are weak, we are
strengthened by an external force that becomes
our own. At the end of her life, Thérèse of
Lisieux offered us this definition of holiness:
"Holiness is not found in a particular practice
but consists of a disposition of the heart which
makes us humble and small in the arms of God,
conscious of our weakness, and boldly confident in his goodness as our Father." I would
like to emphasize these two indissociable com-
ponents: awareness of our weakness and abso-

lute confidence in the goodness and strength of this Father who loves us infinitely. How similar this little Carmelite from Lisieux is to you!

— *Yes, we must accept our weakness, but also admit that, left to ourselves,* **we are nothing***. While I was in the infirmary, prostrating myself during Benediction of the Blessed Sacrament, I prayed to God with all my heart:* **My God, you who are so great, so good, deign to bless such a sinner as I. I worship you. I love you. Have pity on me.**

— It is the prayer of the tax collector that Jesus offers us as an example for us to follow rather than that of the self-righteous Pharisee, who thought he deserved so much (Lk 18:13). When counting our failings, we experience the distance between our ideal self and the mediocrity our lives sometimes reflect. Did St. Paul not suffer the same? "For what I do is not the good I want to do; no, the evil I do not want to do — this I keep on doing ... What a wretched man I am!" (Rm 7:19–24). Humility means opening our eyes to the truth of what we are: "If anyone thinks he is something when he is nothing, he deceives himself" (Gal 6:3). Although Thérèse preached confidence, she did not hesitate to write, "I do not pain myself when I see that I am weakness itself; on the contrary, it is in my weakness that I am glorified ..."

Out of spiritual realism, admitting we are sinners, or, as you said, considering oneself to be "*the last of the Little Sisters*" does not depend on the quantity or enormity of our sins, but on the fact that we are fundamentally incapable of saving ourselves; alone we are incapable of becoming the Saints that God hopes us to become.

When St. Peter walked on water, one wonders whether perhaps for a moment he believed that he himself, through his own powers, was performing such an astonishing feat. Yet, feeling the wind, Peter became afraid. Had he believed that he was walking on water through the powers of the Lord, he would not have become afraid, for it is no more difficult for the Lord to make one walk on troubled waters than on a calm sea. Calling to the Lord to save him, he recognized his weakness as the Lord offered him his hand (Mt 14:25–33). In the same way, admitting our incapacity or our poverty is not discouraging if we have blind faith in the power of the Lord. Paul gloried in his weakness. Like Peter, he experienced his own incapacity, saying, "Three times I pleaded with the Lord to take it away from me. But he said to me, 'My grace is sufficient for you, for my power is made perfect in weakness.' Therefore I will boast all the more gladly about my weaknesses, so that Christ's power may rest on me" (2 Cor 12:8–9). It is this law of God's children that the Blessed Virgin Mary sings of in the Magnificat. She marvels at all the wonders accomplished through God alone, to whom she is just a humble servant.

"My spirit rejoices in God my Savior, for he has been mindful of the lowliness of his servant ... the Almighty has done great things for me. Holy is his name" (Lk 1:47–49).

— *In the foundation and running of our houses,* **we must efface ourselves**, *and carry out his work not for ourselves but for God, accepting that we are but* **his instruments**. *When I think of our first years at Saint-Servan and of the poor, deprived girls we were, it is absolutely obvious that* **it was God who did everything**.

— Dear Sister, you wished to have neither allowance nor fixed revenue and to rely only on Providence. In a similar vein, Thérèse claimed that on a spiritual level, contrary to the Pharisee in the parable, we do not rely on riches or possessions and that "it is necessary to rely on nothing."

I have cited Thérèse a great deal. I recall her visiting your house at Lisieux (founded in 1858), and of her sister Céline painting the portraits of two of your Residents posing in their Sunday best. This visible expression seems only to reinforce your spiritual kinship.

If Thérèse glories in her weakness, she does not cease reminding us to have faith in God: "My path is one of confidence and love." When we think that we are stagnating spiritually, (should we even measure our progress?) would we still become discouraged if we were convinced that

God is capable of everything, that he is the
master of the impossible? This requires total
faith in the Lord. ***Allow yourself to be formed by
God:*** he knows what he wants us to do. When
we are down, we must resist the temptation to
despair and maintain absolute confidence in
God's mercy. Thérèse says, "What pleases God
is to see me love my littleness and nothingness,
to see my blind hope in his mercy," sentiments
that seem to echo your own celebrated words:
**"It is good to be poor, to have nothing, and
depend on God for everything."** Your voices
are different, yet they sing the same song of confidence … When we are faced with a situation
that seems beyond our capacity, if this is what
God wants us to do, we must remind ourselves
that *if God is with us, it will be accomplished*.

I would also add that our "efficacy is God's
own efficacy" (*Poor in Spirit,* p. 81).

Lord, allow us to accept without sadness that
we are poor in virtue and merit! Lord, protector
of the poor, allow us to keep our unwavering
confidence in your merciful love!

Reflection Questions

What are my weaknesses? Can I admit them
to myself? To God? To others? Is there some
area in my spiritual life where I just feel stuck,
unable to make progress? Do I ever feel like "the
good I want to do, I don't do?" Do I become dis-

couraged by my weaknesses and failings, or do I see them as occasions to place my confidence in God? Could I say, with St. Thérèse, "What pleases God is to see me love my littleness and nothingness"? Mary is the perfect model of one who realized that it was God who had done great things in her. How natural is it for me to give God the credit when I experience a consolation or a special grace, or when I achieve something important in life? Do I know how to say, "The Almighty has done great things for me"? Do I stop to thank God for the many graces he has given me?

12

We Were Grafted
into the Cross

Focus Point

////////////

To forget ourselves in order to prefer the will of God to our own will — there can be no greater proof of love. But what about when this renunciation of self leads to suffering and the cross? Even Jesus struggled before he could accept the Father's will, crying out in Gethsemane, "Father, if you are willing, take this cup from me; yet not my will, but yours be done" (Lk 22:42). Ultimately, Jesus accepted the cross as the best means of teaching the world about God's great love for humanity. In the Letter to the Hebrews we read that "Christ learned obedience through what he suffered" (Heb 5:8). For us too, whatever our vocation, obedience to the will of God, and submission to the demands our lives make upon us, can be painful. Yet such submission sets us on a path of love and life, for Jesus promised us that "whoever loses his life for my sake will save it." Lord, help us to believe that, like the grain of wheat that falls into the earth and dies, we too will bear much fruit through our obedience to your holy will.

////////////

In 1877:

"Do not call me Jeanne Jugan. All that is left of her is Sister Mary of the Cross, unworthy though she is of that lovely name."

— When you took your religious name, it marked the beginning of a new life, entirely dedicated to God in service of the poor. This name placed you under the sign of the cross and you could not have imagined to what point the Lord would take you at your word and that you would become like St. Paul: "I have been crucified with Christ and I no longer live, but Christ lives in me" (Gal 2:20).

— *All my life, I placed great value in making the Way of the Cross, meditating at every Station. At the tenth Station, Jesus is stripped of his garments in a call to total poverty — both material and spiritual. At the Eleventh Station, Jesus is nailed to the cross in an act of brutal torture!* **I am attached to the Cross with my Savior, and I want to carry it joyfully until death.**

— You were nailed to the cross from the moment you were demoted from your posi-

tion as Superior (1843) and you stepped aside
without a word. The way you were eclipsed was
reinforced by other humiliations. In 1847, you
did not participate in the General Chapter and
were eliminated from work of any importance.
On December 8, 1854, you pronounced your
perpetual vows, but you were made to wait two
years longer than your first companions and
disciples. Already, you had been relegated to
living among the novices in the motherhouse.
If I may say, it seems that you were treated as
though you did not exist and never had.

Forgive me for evoking these painful memories. I do so since they illustrate so well what
Jesus says about the cross that you were forced
to bear: "If anyone would come after me, he
must deny himself and take up his cross daily
and follow me" (Lk 9:23). In the Gospel it is
clearly written that these words were not being
addressed to future men and women religious,
but to everyone: "Jesus said to them all." Yet
his demand to deny ourselves may make us
afraid. Jesus even speaks of spiritual death
and returns to this on several occasions: "For
whoever wants to save his life will lose it, but
whoever loses his life for my sake will save it"
(Lk 9:24). This is one of many paradoxes in
the Gospel. Obviously, Jesus does not wish to
destroy our personality but to purify it like gold,
"that is perishable even though tested by fire"
(1 Pt 1:7). This renunciation requires us above

all to obey the will of God. In our daily prayers, do we not repeat every day that "Thy will be done" everywhere, beginning with ourselves?

— *I liked singing the hymn that went, "He offers me his cross; yes, I accept, my Savior." We must learn to forget ourselves if we are to make our will the will of God. We cannot offer a greater proof of love.*

— On the evening of Maundy Thursday, Jesus told his Apostles that he would leave them, that he would die. He asked them not to be alarmed even if "the Prince of this world is coming." We understand the frustration his disciples must have felt, that they did not easily accept their broken dreams or the sad, seemingly unavoidable, predictions of their Master. With these words, Jesus quelled their doubts, "But the world must learn that I love the Father and that I do exactly what my Father has commanded me" (Jn 14:31). Accepting the will of the Father could not be done without a painful interior struggle, and several hours later in the Garden of Gethsemane, where Jesus' "Yes" was accompanied by sweat like drops of blood, he cried, "Father, if you are willing, take this cup from me; yet not my will, but yours be done" (Lk 22:42). He pleaded with his disciples to try to understand that by going to the cross, it was so "the world must learn that I love the Father." He addressed his friends, saying, "If you really knew me, you would know my Father as well" (Jn 14:7). Let this supreme testament of Jesus reverberate in our hearts and memories!

— *Jesus obeyed out of love. In religious life, obedience is often painful. This brings to mind a Sister who had spent several happy years in one house and received the nomination from her Superiors to spend time under other skies. Such a change entails a real uprooting, one of many in a lifetime. I explained to her that* **to purify gold, it must first be placed in a furnace, and the dross skimmed and removed from the surface; next it is placed in a second furnace, where the surface must be skimmed less; and finally, it is placed in a third furnace from which it emerges pure and shining.** *The Little Sister could understand that if she embraced these tests as purifications, her love for God would finally sparkle like gold. I also made the comparison of the little stick, explaining to the young Sisters:* **You see my little stick. I move it to the right and to the left and place it before me, yet it never resists. I do as I please with it. We should be like little sticks in the hands of our Superiors.**

— My Sister, allow me to express that I find this view of obedience a little exaggerated. I too wish to be a little stick in the hands of God, and God alone can ask such submission from me. Jesus himself, before accepting the will of his Father, did he not ask him to spare him the trial of the passion and the cross? As human beings, our obedience in religious life and in the Church, cannot be one of a little stick in the hands of God; our obedience must be responsible. Jesus does not treat each of his disciples as servants but as friends: "I no longer call you servants because a servant does not know his master's business. Instead, I have called you friends, for everything that I learned from my Father, I have made known to you" (Jn 15:15). Those who hold some authority remain sister and brother to those who obey them, but might they not forget this?

— *You're right, dear Brother, it is only in the hands of God that we should be like a little stick. In religious life today, obedience is regarded more as a dialogue that will lead us to discover together the will of God ... It is written in our Constitutions.*

— Yes, in the Constitutions it is written, "Dialogue with our Superiors, established in an atmosphere of truth and humility, facilitates true obedience by a surer seeking for the divine will. That is why we may, and sometimes should, humbly and filially expose our opinion, our projects and our difficulties" (*Constitutions,* 49).

This applies all the more so in secular life. God speaks to us through events and people, with or without authority. If through these meditations I can discern what God expects of me, then I obey joyfully and thus make this act of obedience an act of worship and love, thereby making myself part of Jesus' family: "For whoever does the will of my Father in heaven is my brother and sister and mother" (Mt 12:50).

If God's will requires renunciation, it is simply the painful side of the life that Jesus promised us: accepting death in order to live, like the grain of wheat: "I tell you the truth, unless a kernel of wheat falls to the ground and dies, it remains only a single seed. But if it dies, it produces much fruit" (Jn 12:24). The book *The Imitation of Jesus Christ* also speaks about times when life forces us to follow the Way of the cross: "In the cross is life … In the cross is everything, and upon your dying on the cross everything depends. There is no other way to life and to true inward peace than the way of the holy cross" (*The Imitation of Jesus Christ*, Book II, 12). Jesus wants us to live: "I have come that they may have life, and have it to the full" (Jn 10:10). He promises us a life full of plenitude in this world on the condition that we pass through spiritual death. God made us for us to live and be happy. Have faith in him: "Here I am Lord, I have come to do your will."

Reflection Questions

What does the cross mean to me? Is it primarily a symbol of suffering, or of love? Do I run away from suffering, or do I look upon occasions of suffering as opportunities to grow closer to Christ, who offered his life for me? Do I find suffering and joy incompatible? Do I find it hard to obey others, to give in or to sacrifice my own will? Why? When obedience is difficult do I rebel, or do I find peace in Christ's passion? Do I think of myself as a friend of Christ, or as someone who must obey through fear, like a slave? If I see myself as a friend, am I willing to follow Jesus to the cross, to remain with him as Mary and the beloved disciple did? The *Imitation of Christ* says that "There is no other way to life and to true inward peace than the way of the holy cross." Do I really believe this? Do I accept spiritual death as a condition for life with Christ? Do I begin each day with these sentiments, "Here I am, Lord; I come to do your will?"

13
I Will Tell You Three Thoughts

Focus Point

////////////

Jeanne Jugan's advice to the novices was quite practical: to live by faith and to practice charity. In order to do both, faith must be more to us than a set of rules to be observed. Faith is a living relationship with Jesus Christ, the One who gave his life for us and who continues to give himself to us in the Eucharist. When we love others for his sake — no matter who they are — we achieve a unity in our lives because we find Christ in all persons and circumstances. To seek Christ in all things — to find him in prayer and to serve him in the person of the poor — this is the recipe for a fruitful life. Lord, teach us to love others as you love them; in this way the world will recognize us as your disciples.

////////////

"I'm going to tell you three thoughts; if you make them part of your life, you will become a great Saint: the just man lives by faith; charity covers a multitude of sins, and she who keeps guard over her tongue keeps guard over her soul."

— You, my Sister, took these three thoughts, originating from the Old Testament and taken up in the New, and transformed them into a sort of program. If you have given them such emphasis, it is because your experience has shown you their importance as a guide for daily life.

— *Our poverty obliged us to live by faith. Some live in security because their bank accounts clearly show that they have savings. We, on the other hand, had invisible credit with the Good God. Our security came from our faith, and if our faith had weakened, we would have become discouraged.*

— When St. Paul said, "The righteous will live by faith" (Rm 1:17), he was quoting the Prophet Habakkuk (Hb 2:4). One could also interpret this as "the just live by fidelity," but what is fidelity but faith that withstands the test of time? After the excitement of the engagement, fidelity demonstrates that one's initial faith has not been shaken. All of these words have the same root as faith, and so do the sentiments they evoke!

Your faith was not simply a matter of adhering to a set of truths; above all, you emphasized that you had faith in Someone. Jesus, who before giving us the Eucharist, asks us to believe in him, "He who believes in me will never be thirsty … everyone who looks to the Son and believes in him shall have eternal life" (Jn 6:35–40); and in the hours that precede his Passion, he seems to beseech us when he says, "Trust in God; trust also in me" (Jn 14:1). Cardinal Garrone comments on this by saying, "Believing in Jesus Christ means giving ourselves with all our soul, in trust, in humility, in love, in adoration and in service, to him whom we acknowledge as Lord…. He is our God become our brother" (*Poor in Spirit,* p. 58).

If our faith is alive, Jesus has an important place in our lives. We feel his presence in the same way that we sense people who are visible around us. We listen to him, talk to him … he is everywhere: "I believe in Jesus Christ. Whoever says this with all his heart and all his mind and all his soul has said all that there is to be said" (*Poor in Spirit,* p. 58).

— *Yes, all has been said. And when an elderly person needs our care, we do not leave the Lord, for in caring for this person, we are taking care of Christ, even when it prevents us from going to the chapel. I remember this principle of the Society of the Admirable Mother, where a young girl was excused from going "to church or religious ceremonies when her presence was needed elsewhere." That was a long time ago, but for me, charity has always taken pre-cedence. This makes me think of a novice who hesi-tated to leave the recitation of the rosary when she was needed elsewhere for pressing work: I assured her with these words,* **"Go quickly, it is more perfect to obey than to pray to the good God."**

— In this precise case, there was no fault—on the contrary. I say this since you cite the ancient maxim of St. Peter: "Love covers over a multitude of sins" (1 Pt 4:8). St. Paul and St. James speak in the same vein. In the Gospel, we witness the scene of Jesus welcoming a weeping sinner with benevolence, saying, "Her many sins have been forgiven—for she loved much" (Lk 7:47). It is on our love that we will be judged.

— *I also asked to keep guard over one's tongue because it is a domain in which it is easy to be unchari-table. In the Book of Proverbs, it is written, "He who guards his lips guards his life, but he who speaks rashly will come to ruin" (Prv 13:3).* **A Little Sister must never fail in charity in anything she says.** *I have always been uncompromising about this.*

— Jesus asks us never to judge, advice which concludes several Parables, including the Parable of the Weeds (Mt 13:24). Judgement is reserved for him alone and this at the end of time. As for St. James, he dedicates a whole passage to taming the tongue (Jas 3:1–12).

— It is in charity that we can recognize Jesus' disciples. He told us this insistently on Holy Thursday after the Last Supper: "As I have loved you, so you must love one another. By this all men will know that you are my disciples, if you love one another" (Jn 13:34–35). We will never be good enough, we will never resemble him enough!

— Is this not what non-Christians expect from us? In your day, for example, there weren't many Muslims in Brittany, but very quickly you established a House in Algeria, the first, in Algiers, being founded by Cardinal Lavigerie in 1868. Muslims are familiar with these words that the Koran places in the mouth of God: "Then, after the prophets we sent Jesus son of Mary, and gave him the Gospel. And we ordained in the hearts of those who followed him, compassion and mercy" (Surah 57, Verse 27). Consequently, Muslims hope to find kindness and friendship among Christians; they expect from them expressions of real charity. Your Little Sisters, who went all over the world, must have had hearts open to love every human being, regardless of race or religion.

*— Even in our homes in Europe, there weren't only devout Christians. The Little Sisters were saddened by this and made efforts to win over to our religion those who did not practice. I asked them to be very discreet. **Instead of insisting, it is better to wait for God's hour to come.***

— Father Lelièvre thought like you. In a letter describing the sometimes sorrowful physical and mental state of the elderly, he acknowledged that they are the "object of our preference. It would be impertinent and cruel on our part to preach to them."

— *It would be so wonderful if the way we lived our lives made others think of the Good God!*

— Father de Foucauld wrote in his diary, "If I were asked why I am gentle and good, I would say it is because I am the servant of a higher cause. If only you knew how good my Master Jesus is!" Our behavior may provoke questions in those around us, even though they may not express them verbally. Your three thoughts, dear Sister, have trained us to speak once again of charity. You felt very strongly about this. How can we summarize these thoughts?

— *I can only tell you once again what I kept saying to the novices, but it applies to all Christians, doesn't it?* **To be a good Little Sister of the Poor, one must love God and the poor a great deal, and forget oneself.**

— Of course! And just because the words are simple does not mean that this is easy!

Reflection Questions

Is my faith realized through a personal, living relationship with Christ, or is it merely the following of a set of rules? It has been said that believing in Jesus means giving ourselves with all our heart, in adoration, trust and service. Is my self-gift complete? If not, what am I withholding from Jesus? Do I sometimes feel that I just can't do it all — work, family obligations, faith practices, prayer, service? Do I get so caught up in noise and activity that I am unable to discern God's presence and his will in the various facets of my life? Could I learn to find unity in him through regular prayer? Do I have a good balance between prayer and action, or do I tend to overemphasize one at the expense of the other? How good am I at controlling my tongue? Do I tend to judge others, or to look upon them charitably? Do I live my Christian faith in such a way that my behavior provokes questions in others, or even opens their minds and hearts to God? Am I ready to give an account for the hope that is in me? (1 Pt 3:15).

14

See How Jesus, Mary and Joseph Loved One Another

Focus Point

The Holy Family of Nazareth has much to teach us — docility to God's plan and obedience to his Word, union of hearts in charity, humility, simplicity, the value of work as the daily expression of love and the importance of the interior life. Perhaps the greatest thing they can teach us is that goodness works quietly, and that holiness can be found in the ordinary events of everyday life. St. Joseph, the patron and protector of the Little Sisters, gives an especially powerful witness of these truths. In his apostolic letter, *Redemptoris Custos,* Pope John Paul II quoted his predecessor Pope Pius XII, who once said, "St. Joseph is the model of those humble ones that Christianity raises up to great destinies; ... he is the proof that in order to be a good and genuine follower of Christ, there is no need of great things — it is enough to have the common, simple and human virtues, but they need to be true and authentic" (R.C., 24). Lord, help us to live as the Holy Family and to follow St. Joseph's example of love and service.

///////////

"See how Jesus, Mary and Joseph loved one another, all three, how happy they looked, with what kindness they spoke to each other. In our little family, it must be the same. We must love one another like them."

— My Sister, I see that the place you give the Holy Family is very much in line with the Eudist spirituality of your youth. As you said so well, Nazareth should inspire mutual love in our communities, and if I may add, in all communities and in all families. Each member of the Holy Family was attentive to the others, and sought to make the others happy.

Yet the Gospel tells us almost nothing about the life of the Holy Family since it was very much an ordinary life, and Jesus wanted so much to be an ordinary man! Imagine how many other families God could have chosen; we should admire the fact that he chose the one from Nazareth. We cannot meditate enough on the mystery of the Incarnation, not only on the prodigious event itself, but also on how it occurred: "Who, being in very nature God, did not consider equality with God something to be grasped, but he emptied himself, taking the form of a slave, being made in human likeness. And being found in human appearance, he humbled himself and became obedient to death — even death on a cross!" (Phil 2:6–8).

After the episode at the Temple, the Gospel summarizes the childhood and adolescence of Jesus in one single line: "Then he went down to Nazareth with them and was obedient to them. But his mother treasured all these things in her heart" (Lk 2:51). Charles Péguy commented admirably on this: "Obedience, Jesus' submission to his earthly parents, so perfect in itself and eternal in its teaching, was only a temporal image, a bodily representation of Jesus' eternal filial obedience to his Father in Heaven. Obedience, Jesus' daily submission to Mary and Joseph foretold, represented and anticipated the alarming obedience and submission he demonstrated on Holy Thursday."[3]

— *Dear Brother, in their life in Nazareth, there was not only great harmony among the three of them, but they also worked closely together. It is also through work that our homes should reflect the life of the Holy Family.* **The Holy Virgin was poor: she teaches us order and cleanliness ... because if there is no order or cleanliness, poverty is not taken care of. The Holy Virgin was like the poor, she did not waste her time since the poor are not idle: in this, we must imitate the Holy Family.**

— Jesus was the village carpenter. He crafted beams, cabinets, and even ploughs in a workshop where the Word of God was silent. What greatness there is in manual work! "Through him all things were made" (Jn 1:3), yet Jesus wanted to learn his craft through Joseph. In contemplating the painting of the workshop in Nazareth, one can sense something of the incredible and mysterious humility of God. One sees Jesus carrying planks of wood on his shoulder, and Jesus washing the feet of his Apostles, images of God among us that go against any ideas we may have of God. When we question ourselves about what seems disconcerting or unreasonable in God's ways, only one explanation seems satisfying: He behaves this way because he loves us. And love, as we know, is sometimes foolish. What measure can exist between our earthly loves and the follies of God's love? Who will probe the infinite abyss of his heart? The more love there is in our hearts, the more we can sense this extraordinary divine love. St. Paul wishes the following for us: "I pray that you, being rooted and established in love, may have power, together with all the Saints, to grasp how wide and long and high and deep is the love of Christ, and to know this love that surpasses knowledge" (Eph 3:17–19).

Returning to life in Nazareth, Father de Foucauld thought that Christians "should try to resemble Our Lord Jesus more and more, taking as model his life in Nazareth, which provides us with innumerable examples." Whether in his garden shed in Nazareth or with his Saharan brotherhood, Father de Foucauld led a family life with Jesus, Mary and Joseph.

The latter, the most humble of the three, is held in great esteem by your Little Sisters. He is the patron and protector of the Congregation and presides over your homes and Motherhouse.

In 1856, the Little Sisters acquired an old manor with woods, meadows, workable land, and ponds at La Tour in the commune of Saint-Pern (Ille-et-Vilaine). Three Little Sisters from the house at Rennes arrived at La Tour on April 1st, which in that year marked the feast of St. Joseph; it is therefore only natural that the property would be named La Tour St. Joseph. Several years later, a statue of St. Joseph was placed atop the 54-meter-high steeple of the chapel, overlooking the imposing buildings of the manor, as a symbol of his role as guardian of the motherhouse and all the Little Sisters and Residents all over the world.

— *I always had absolute confidence in this great patriarch as protector and provider of the spiritual and temporal well-being of our little family. I had prayers offered through his intercession everywhere. When we lacked food or clothing, we confided our worries to him. He, our foster father, always made sure that the Virgin Mary and Jesus had the necessities in life, and he took care of us in the same way.*

— This unfailing devotion to St. Joseph is characteristic of the Little Sisters' spirituality. And they certainly keep him busy with a great deal of work!

Nowadays, such confidence might seem quite surprising or might simply make us smile. Perhaps one needs the heart of a child to understand it. On this point, you are of the same school as St. Teresa of Avila, doctor of the Church, who writes, "To other saints the Lord seems to have given a grace to help us in some of our necessities, but of this glorious saint (St. Joseph) my experience is that he helps us in them all and that the Lord wishes to teach us that as he was himself subject to him on earth (for, being his guardian and being called his father, he could command him) just so in Heaven, he still does all that Jesus asks."

Dear Sister, allow me to add that St. Joseph seems to have been a man of few words. There is not one word of his to be found in the four Gospels. Can we hope that by spending time with him, we can learn to speak less?

If we are attentive to the liturgy, we ask God to unify all members of the great family of humanity: "Father, help us to live as a holy family, united in respect and love. Bring us to the joy and peace of your eternal home."

Reflection Questions

A well-known passage in the Second Book of Kings (chapt. 5), tells the story of Naaman, who is told by a prophet to wash in the Jordan River in order to cure his leprosy. Naaman becomes upset at the ordinariness of this proposal because he was expecting something much more spectacular. Do I sometimes unrealistically expect God to intervene in extraordinary ways, rather than accepting his quiet, hidden activity in my life? Do I look for the flashy, the showy or even the miraculous? Do I have a hard time understanding a God who emptied himself, taking the form of a slave? What about when he asks me to follow him in this self-emptying? Do I have a hard time obeying God or his intermediaries (my parents, superiors or others in positions of authority) when what he is asking of me does not seem to make sense? Do I value simple work? What about silence? Do I know how to sacrifice my own interests or goals in order to live in charity and unity with my family, roommates or religious community?

15

The Hail Mary Will Take Us to Heaven

Focus Point

////////////

As he was dying on the Cross, Jesus confided his most precious possession to us: "Behold your mother." Mary has thus always been the mother of all believers. In authentic Marian devotion, our affection for Mary is inspired by our relationship with Jesus. When we turn to Mary, she, in turn, leads us to Jesus. The example of Mary's life also inspires us in our pursuit of Christian holiness: in the Annunciation we see Mary's faith and obedience; in the Visitation we are motivated by her apostolic charity. Through her fidelity to her Son's mission and her courage in standing beneath the Cross she showed herself to be the first and most faithful disciple. Finally, Mary was a soul of prayer in the heart of the young church. By following

Mary's example we too hope to arrive one day in Heaven, where we will join in our Mother's eternal Magnificat, her song of praise for the mercies of God. Mary, you know that we love you and long to see you; intercede for us with your Son now and at the hour of our death.

//////////////

"You love Our Lady. She will be your Mother."

"Say the Memorare and say it often. You can never say it enough: Remember, O Most Gracious Virgin Mary, that never was it known that anyone who fled to your protection, implored your help or sought your intercession was left unaided."

— My Sister, you carried your rosary in your hand when you went begging in the streets and you continued to carry it while you walked in the gardens of the novitiate, where you prayed before the statue of the Blessed Virgin. You spent a lot of time each day praying the rosary.

*— I wanted the Little Sisters to pray a great deal to the Blessed Virgin, sure that **the Hail Mary will take us to heaven**. When a novice would bring me fresh linen or wood for the fire, I would thank her by saying a Hail Mary or two with her. It's not good to recite the rosary mechanically. As much as possible, one should pray it while meditating the mysteries, so*

that our devotion does not separate Jesus Christ from his Mother, who orients us towards him. At Cana, the Blessed Virgin recommended us to "do whatever he tells you."

— You just showed us the spirit of authentic Marian devotion. Mary should not hide Jesus from us; but the inverse is also true: Jesus should not hide Mary from us. In reaction to certain deviations and excesses of Marian devotion in the postconciliary years, some tried to reduce it to almost nothing. Far from such excesses, let our affection for the Blessed Virgin take its inspiration from Jesus, the Son *par excellence*. We, her other children, should take the eldest Son as our model.

Jesus wished his new family to be a spiritual one founded on faith. We can be a member of this family if we carry out the will of our Father in Heaven (Mt 12:50). We see that on Jesus' death, Mary becomes the mother of his brothers according to the faith, and Jesus entrusts her to John rather than to a member of his own family, which would have been usual at the time.

— Is this not remarkable?

— *As you have just said through this passage of the Gospel, Mary is truly my mother. We must turn towards her. From the cradle to the cross, she did not cease to contemplate her Son. Our prayers can pass through her, even though they are addressed to Jesus.*

I taught the novices to express themselves in this manner: "O! Blessed Virgin, Allow that our prayers are received by him who was born of you."

— Besides, dear Sister, in the Ave Maria, it is not to the Blessed Virgin that we pray — we ask her to pray for us, poor sinners. The same can be said for the ejaculation in honor of the Immaculate Conception: "O Mary, conceived without sin, pray for us who have recourse to thee."

The Second Vatican Council strongly insisted on the mediation of Jesus Christ, who is the "sole Mediator," and referred us to the words of St. Paul: "For there is one God and one mediator between God and men, the man Christ Jesus, who gave himself as a ransom for all men" (1 Tm 2:5–6). One must keep this truth present in our minds to be able to situate the role of the Virgin Mary in its rightful place. The Council warned, "For no creature could ever be counted as equal with the Incarnate Word and Redeemer" (*Lumen Gentium*, 62). Mary is a human creature, not a goddess. A young woman from Galilee, chosen by God among all women, she lived in faith, which brings her so close to us that we can address her as a mother. "True devotion ... proceeds from true faith, by which we are led to know the excellence of the Mother of God, and we are moved to a filial love toward our mother and to the imitation of her virtues" (*Lumen Gentium*). Mary, although discreet in the

Gospel, is always united with her son, and in her right place, she pleads and intercedes on behalf of us. Many titles have been given to her, such as Mother and Model of the Church, Cause of Our Joy, Comforter of the Afflicted, Queen of Peace, etc.

The Mystery of the Visitation may inspire our apostolic path. Just as Mary went to see her cousin Elizabeth, so do we approach others, like her, with Christ alive in our hearts. Through our words and actions, we can become transparent to this invisible presence!

At the Annunciation, the Angel Gabriel addresses Mary with "full of grace." In every Hail Mary, we repeat this greeting to her who is loved and favored by God through her Immaculate Conception.

— *You know that since the beginning of the Congregation, our religious profession has been made "in the presence of Mary Immaculate." And we, my companions and I, decided to renew our vows every year on December 8th, the Feast of the Immaculate Conception, a tradition that the Little Sisters have kept alive until today. Later, when the chapel at Dinan was built, we dedicated it to Mary Immaculate. This was in 1854, four years before the Virgin Mary presented herself as the Immaculate Conception to Bernadette, a humble visionary, at Lourdes.*

As I have already said, I always enjoyed singing and having sung one of my favorite hymns, "O!

Bonne Mère" in honor of the Virgin Mary. Each verse ends with the line, "Close my eyes yourself, O! Bonne Mère." At my age — I'm over eighty — it's not surprising that I attach such importance to these words!

— The Holy Virgin has heard you and will be very much present at your death. You never stopped saying to her, **"O Mary, you know that you are my mother. Do not abandon me!"**

One fine day, you left your straw hat and clogs, placed your stick in the corner, and stretched out your body in a bed in the infirmary, still with your rosary between your fingers. In recent years, you have been almost blind, but soon you will see forever! One of your last prayers, addressed to Our Lord was, **"Eternal Father, open your gates today to the most miserable of your children, but one who greatly longs to see you."** And one heard you murmur, **"O Mary, my dear Mother, come to me. You know that I love you and that I long to see you."** Your desire to finally see your dear Mother and Our Lord in Heaven was quickly granted, since, with your last breath, your face illuminated with a great smile.

Now, I would like to sing with you the Magnificat. The Lord looked with tenderness upon the humble condition of the first Little Sister of the Poor. Through her and with her, he accomplished many wonders, multiplied by all the other Little Sisters around the world, through whom he has been able to feed thousands of his poor. This is why you have been declared Saint. She who was relegated and unrecognized is now being venerated for her work!

In truth, the Song of Mary can become your own. A humble servant, like her, you can proclaim, "The Almighty has done great things for me and holy is his name. He has mercy on those who fear him, from generation to generation. He has shown strength with his arm and has scattered the proud … lifting up the lowly … He has filled the hungry with good things … He has come to the aid of his servant Israel, to remember his promise of mercy."

Reflection Questions

Am I too "grown-up" and sophisticated to accept the help of a mother? If I have no devotion to Mary, why not? If I do, does my devotion to the Mother of God lead me closer to the Lord himself? Do I take time for the rosary? Do I rush through it, or do I use it as a means of meditation and contemplation on the life of Christ? Do I find the rosary to be beneficial in my spiritual life? Can I identify with Mary as a model of discipleship? Mary lived in faith and served her neighbor with the eagerness of love. Where do I stand in faith and love? Can I, like Mary, recognize the wonders the Almighty has done for me? How often do I think to thank him, to bless his holy name? Do I long for heaven?

Bibliography

Two Biographies:

— *Jeanne Jugan, Sister Mary of the Cross — Foundress of the Institute of the Little Sisters of the Poor.* Monsignor Francis Trochu, La Tour Saint-Joseph, 1961.

— *Jeanne Jugan, Humble So As to Love More.* Paul Milcent, Darton, Longman and Todd, London, 1978–1996; available from the Publications Office, Little Sisters of the Poor.

And a booklet on a collaborator of the Little Sisters:

— *Ernest Lelièvre* (1826–1889), Publications Office, Little Sisters of the Poor.

Three beautiful meditations on her life and message:

— *Poor in Spirit.* Cardinal Gabriel-Marie Garrone, Darton, Longman and Todd, London, 1993; available from the Publications Office, Little Sisters of the Poor.

139

— *Jeanne Jugan, The Desert and the Rose*. Éloi Leclerc, Darton, Longman and Todd, London, 2000; available from the Publications Office, Little Sisters of the Poor.

— *Sayings of Jeanne Jugan,* Sr. Elizabeth Allard, Publications Office, Little Sisters of the Poor.

A magazine:

Serenity, Little Sisters of the Poor quarterly bulletin.

Subscriptions: Little Sisters of the Poor, Publications Office, Baltimore, MD 21228.

Address of the U.S. Publications Office
of the Little Sisters of the Poor:

Little Sisters of the Poor
Publications Office
601 Maiden Choice Lane
Baltimore, MD 21228

Notes

1 Translated from A. Peyriguère, *Laissez-vous saisir par le Christ*, "Livre de Vie" collection, Editions Seuil, p. 30.

2 Translated from *Écrits spirituels* by Elizabeth of the Trinity, Editions du Seuil, p. 203, p. 135.

3 Translated from *Un nouveau théologien. M. Laudet.*

Also available in the
"15 Days of Prayer" series:

Saint Augustine *(Jaime García)*
978-0-7648-0655-6, paper

Saint Benedict *(André Gozier)*
978-1-56548-304-0, paper

Saint Bernadette of Lourdes *(François Vayne)*
978-1-56548-314-9, paper

Saint Bernard *(Emery Pierre-Yves)*
978-0764-805745, paper

Dietrich Bonhoeffer *(Matthieu Arnold)*
978-1-56548-311-8, paper

Saint Catherine of Siena *(Chantal van der
   Plancke and Andrè Knockaert)*
978-156548-310-1, paper

Pierre Teilhard de Chardin *(André Dupleix)*
978-0764-804908, paper

The Curé of Ars *(Pierre Blanc)*
978-0764-807138, paper

Saint Dominic *(Alain Quilici)*
978-0764-807169, paper

Saint Katharine Drexel *(Leo Luke Marcello)*
978-0764-809231, paper

Don Bosco *(Robert Schiele)*
978-0764-807121, paper

Charles de Foucauld *(Michael Lafon)*
978-0764-804892, paper

Saint Francis de Sales *(Claude Morel)*
978-0764-805752, paper

Saint Francis of Assisi *(Thaddée Matura)*
978-1-56548-315-6, paper

Saint John of the Cross *(Constant Tonnelier)*
978-0764-806544, paper

Saint Eugene de Mazenod *(Bernard Dullier)*
978-1-56548-320-0, paper

Saint Louis de Montfort *(Veronica Pinardon)*
978-0764-807152, paper

Henri Nouwen *(Robert Waldron)*
978-1-56548-324-8, paper

Saint Martín de Porres: A Saint of the Americas *(Brian J. Pierce)*
978-0764-812163, paper

Meister Eckhart *(André Gozier)*
978-0764-806520, paper

Thomas Merton *(André Gozier)*
978-0764-804915, paper

Saint Elizabeth Ann Seton *(Betty Ann McNeil)*
978-0764-808418, paper

Johannes Tauler *(André Pinet)*
978-0764-806537, paper

Saint Teresa of Ávila *(Jean Abiven)*
978-0764-805738, paper

Saint Thomas Aquinas *(André Pinet)*
978-0764-806568, paper